Battleground Europe

FROMELLES

Battleground Europe

FROMELLES

Peter Pedersen

To my Father and in loving memory of my Mother

Series editor
Nigel Cave

LEO COOPER

Cover: *Battle of Fromelles* by Charles Wheeler (AWM ART 07981)

Other books by Peter Pedersen:
Monash as Military Commander
Images of Gallipoli
Hamel (Battleground Europe Series)

First published in 2004 by
LEO COOPER
an imprint of
Pen & Sword Books Limited
47 Church Street, Barnsley, South Yorkshire S70 2AS

ISBN 0 85052 928 X

A CIP catalogue of this book is available
from the British Library

Printed by CPI UK

For up-to-date information on other titles produced under the Leo Cooper imprint,
please telephone or write to:

Pen & Sword Books Ltd, FREEPOST, 47 Church Street
Barnsley, South Yorkshire S70 2AS
Telephone 01226 734222

CONTENTS

Introduction by the Series Editor

The sweep of country below Messines Ridge to the heights of Notre Dame de Lorette and Vimy Ridge seems unremitting in its flatness and lack of features. How much more so must this have seemed to the soldiers after the destruction wrought in the area of the Front Line in the fighting of 1914 and 1915. And what a contrast, in particular, for those Australian soldiers who had seen action in the arid and rugged terrain of Gallipoli.

This is the area of France that presented the country's weak northern front to potential foes, the one part that France's foreign policy, spearheaded by Cardinal Richelieu in the early seventeenth century, had been unable to secure with natural frontiers, such as those of the Rhine to the east and the Alps and the Pyrenees to the south.

It was here that much of the British army's offensive action took place in 1915 – at Neuve Chapelle, Festubert and Aubers Ridge in the spring of 1915 and at Loos in the autumn. And then this sector fell silent, as the fight moved south to the Somme and the Hindenburg Line, or north to Messines and the Salient. It was to be undisturbed until the German offensive on the Lys in 1918 and the British Advance to Victory in the autumn of that year. Undisturbed, that is, except for the tragic battle of Fromelles in July 1916, almost ignored by British accounts of the war as the Somme battle raged, but of enormous significance to the Australians, representing as it did the first ANZAC battle on the Western Front.

This is a dismal story of a battle that need never have been fought, that was rushed in planning and had only the redeeming grace of the men who fought so bravely in it. These men deserve to have their story told and have their actions put on the ground; deserve to have visitors who visit their graves knowing something about why and how so many of them who lie buried in these cemeteries met their premature end.

As an aside, it is also an area which to my mind has one of the most beautiful – if not the most beautiful – Commonwealth War Graves Cemeteries in France; Le Trou Aid Post, especially in late spring and early summer, is an enchanting place, where even the sadness inspired by the lines of graves cannot take away from a realisation of the potential of humankind's creativity.

Nigel Cave
Porta Latina, Rome

AUTHOR'S INTRODUCTION

Private Charles William Johnston, 56 Battalion, Australian Imperial Force (AIF), fell in the attack at Fromelles on 19 July 1916. A brilliant student who became a highly regarded teacher, he had touched many lives and his passing was widely felt. His grief-stricken parents, who lost a second son on the Somme later that year, could not bear to tell their other children that Charles was never found. As far as his sister Margaret knew, he rested in a war grave in France. Curious, her son enquired with the Office of Australian War Graves and found out that Charles was commemorated on the wall of VC Corner Australian Cemetery in the old No Man's Land. Her grandson subsequently visited it. Naturally, nothing was said to Margaret, who remained unaware of the truth to the end of her life. Fromelles had affected three generations. I am Margaret Johnston's grandson. Charles Johnston was my great uncle.

Private Charles Johnston.

The attack was intended to prevent the Germans reinforcing the Somme front, where the great British offensive had been underway since 1 July, with units from the quiet Fromelles sector near Lille. Its story makes depressing reading. In one night, the 5th Australian Division lost 5,533 men and was crippled as a fighting formation for several months. The British 61st Division alongside it was also badly mauled. Both divisions were dreadfully inexperienced – indeed, the battle was the AIF's first major action on the Western Front.

Inexperience, though, was not the only reason why the chances of success were practically zero from the start. Veteran divisions had been thrown back with appalling losses when assaulting over this ground in May 1915 and, if the German line was formidable then, it had been improved since. Some of the senior commanders were involved in both battles but their planning for the second took little account of what had happened in the first. The Australian general was no military paragon either. His men were bewildered by the haste and confusion that blighted the lead-up.

The one redeeming feature was the courage shown at the sharp end. Where No Man's Land was at its widest, almost 400 metres across, the Australian and British infantrymen did not hesitate in the face of torrential fire and were shot down in droves. Where it was narrower, the Australians held the German line until a lack of ammunition and dwindling numbers forced them to withdraw. For days afterward, they went out to recover their wounded. As the defence was masterly, the Germans have to be given their due as well. A certain Adolf Hitler was among them.

On the battlefield little has changed and the Australian sector, where the fighting was prolonged, is very accessible. As VC Corner Australian Cemetery rarely passes from view and some of the other cemeteries are within easy walking distance, the cost of courage is always evident. Which is exactly as it should be.

P.A. Pedersen
Sydney, Australia

ACKNOWLEDGEMENTS

This book could not have been written without the unstinting support of my father during the part of each year that I spend at my desk in Sydney. Dad, I owe you more than I can say.

In France, Martial Delebarre, the Official Secretary of the *Association Souvenir de la Bataille de Fromelles* (ASBF) and curator of its museum, arranged for me to see those areas of the battlefield that are on private land and took me underground at the ASBF's ongoing archeological projects. He also provided many period photographs and answered a barrage of queries. Martial's ASBF colleague, Benoît DeLattre, and Bernard's father Francis, a former mayor of Fromelles, lent enthusiastic support. So did Jacques Follet and Diane Melloy Follet. I appreciated the perspective of my colleague Jon Cooksey, with whom I spent many enjoyable hours walking the area. Jon helped out too, when some photographs went astray!

In Australia, the staff of the Australian War Memorial bent over backwards to help. Special thanks to Ian Smith, Senior Curator of Official and Private Records; Bill Fogarty, Senior Curator of Photographs, Film and Sound; and Anne-Marie Conde, the Reading Room Manager. Claudia Krebs of the Office of Australian War Graves cheerfully sent information on cemeteries and graves. No request was too great for Ursula Davidson, Librarian at the Royal United Service Institution of New South Wales. Harry Taplin put his extensive German archive at my disposal. Robin Corfield was also very helpful.

In England, Richard Jeffs of the Oxfordshire and Buckinghamshire Light Infantry Museum gave me a wealth of information and read parts of the manuscript. I would also like to record the assistance of the Royal Regiment of Fusiliers and the Soldiers of Gloucestershire Museums and the Reading Room staff at the Imperial War Museum and the Public Record Office in London.

ADVICE TO TRAVELLERS

The Fromelles battlefield is several kilometres south of Armentières. To get there from Calais, head east from the ferry terminal on the A16-E40 Autoroute to junction 28 and then south on the N225, which soon becomes the A25. At junction 7, take the D7 for La Bassée and turn right after a couple of kilometres onto the D141B, which reaches Fromelles after passing through the village of le Maisnil. Visitors coming from Ypres on the N336/N365 can avoid the tangle of roads around Armentières by turning right in the centre of Ploegsteert and continuing westwards through Romarin to the D933. Turn left onto it, following the signs for Nieppe and Armentières. After 3 kilometres turn right onto the access road for junction 9 of the A25-E42 Autoroute and head left on reaching it. Once on the A25, the directions are the same as for the drive from Calais.

Before leaving, check that you have appropriate vehicle cover. Full personal insurance is also strongly recommended. Take an E111 Form, obtainable from your post office, for reciprocal medical and hospital cover in France and make sure your tetanus vaccination is current. A hat, waterproof smock and sun cream are essential as the sun can be scorching, shade is at premium and rain falls at any time. Do not forget binoculars because the battlefield is totally flat and picking out locations is difficult without them. A compass will help you orient the maps in this book to the ground. Good hiking shoes or boots are a must.

Remember that the area is a farming community and the locals get restless when unthinking visitors tramp across their fields. Stay on the farm tracks and the edges of the fields and, if in doubt, ask. Be careful if the crops have been harvested because lines of men equipped for the gunfight at the OK Corral will be blasting the rabbits and anything else that moves to smithereens. Drivers should be careful not to obstruct agricultural vehicles, which is easy to do on the narrow roads. Leave any dud ammunition you see well alone.

Allow time for a visit to the museum on the second floor of the town hall on the Rue de Verdun in Fromelles. It is perhaps the best small museum on the Western Front and explains not just the battles of

Fromelles and Aubers Ridge but also the course of the war in the area. Most of the relics have been recovered by the ASBF, which operates the museum and has carried out extensive archeological work on the battlefield since its establishment in 1988. They range from pumping machinery found in British dugouts and specialised equipment taken from German mine galleries to soldiers' personal items. Opening hours are 9 am-12 pm and 2-7 pm on every second Sunday between April-December, excluding August. Visits at other times can be arranged by calling the Mairie (03-20-502043) three weeks in advance during office hours. The ASBF's website is www.asbf14-18.org.

While Armentières offers a range of accommodation, the choices for those wishing to stay locally are limited. The following bed and breakfasts are close to the battlefield:

La Louisane, 51 Rue des Sablonnières, 59249 AUBERS
Tel: 33 320 50 20 42

Chez Julie, 8 Rue de Radinghem, 59134 BEAUCAMPS-LIGNY
Tel: 33 320 50 33 82; ctilmant@wanadoo.fr

Ferme de Rosembois, Hameau du Bas Flandres, 59134 FOURNES-EN-WEPPES
Tel: 33 320 50 25 69

Chambres de la Pépinière, 59 Rue du Riez, 59134 HERLIES
Tel: 33 320 29 80 70

Relais des Weppes, 40 Rue du Riez, 59134 HERLIES
Tel: 33 320 29 13 54

MAPS

The Fromelles battlefield is frustratingly split between two 1:10,000 series trench maps, ninety percent of it lying on the Aubers sheet and the remaining ten percent on the Radinghem sheet. Reflecting GHQ security concerns in 1916, the editions current at the time of the battle omitted every detail of the British defences apart from the course of the front line. Making matters worse, place names are sometimes spelled differently on the trench maps than they are on modern maps.

As British maps were fully detailed after 1916, I have used editions that postdate the battle: Aubers, Sheet 36 SW1, Edition 10A, correct as at 1 January 1918, and Radinghem Sheet 36 SW2, Edition 10A, correct as at 19 December 1917. Before the purists start having palpitations, I would point out that the lines hardly changed in the

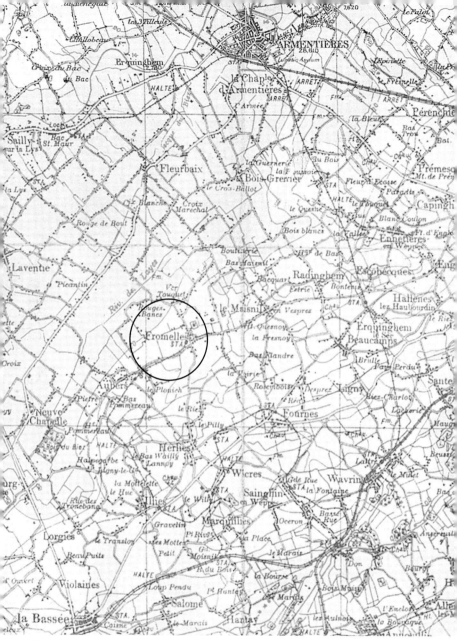

Area map.

Fromelles-Aubers area throughout the war. The later maps also show the 300-Yard Line and the communication trenches that were so important. Both maps should be available from the Department of

11

Printed Books at the Imperial War Museum in London (0171-416-5348) or the Western Front Association – if you are a member.

Locations on the trench maps have been given according to the reference system used at the time. Maps were divided into squares covering an area of 6,000 yards by 6,000 yards. Each was identified by a letter of the alphabet – mainly N in the case of the Fromelles battlefield – and further subdivided into six rows of six squares, making a total of 36 consecutively numbered squares each measuring 1,000 by 1,000 yards. Every one of these squares was broken down into four smaller sub-squares that were lettered clockwise as a,b,d,c. The eastings and northings in each sub-square were then subdivided in intervals of ten and marked off thus on two sides. As an example, the German line crossed the Rue Delvas at N.9.d.4.1 – the location of the Australian Memorial Park.

The relevant IGN Blue Series 1:25,000 map, which you will find useful for the driving tour, is Sheet 2404E (Armentières). It can be obtained from Waterstone's Booksellers in the UK, Maison de la Press shops or major supermarkets in France, or by online order from IGN at www.ign.fr.

HOW TO USE THIS BOOK

As a debacle was likely at Fromelles before a shot had been fired, the plan and the preparations for the attack should be grasped thoroughly in order to get the most out of the battle narratives. As you read, try to see the battlefield in your mind's eye, which will give you a head start when you embark on the tours suggested in Chapter Nine. Ideally, complete the drive first so that you know where the principal locations are in relation to each other before you undertake the more detailed walks.

Similarly, if you are focusing on the action in a particular part of the battlefield, put it within the context of what was happening elsewhere, otherwise your study will lack coherence. This advice is particularly relevant to the assault either side of the interdivisional boundary and the fighting early on the morning of 20 July that led to the Australian withdrawal.

Finally, remember the soldiers. Wherever possible, this guide has let them say what they thought, felt and saw. Use your imagination to bring their words alive and you will have some idea of what fighting at Fromelles was like. Besides having a technical understanding of the battle, you will also gain an appreciation of the battlefield as a place where ordinary men achieved great things.

Chapter One

DEFENDING FROMELLES: THE GERMANS

Seventeen miles south of Ypres and six south of Armentières, Fromelles dates from Roman times, although its recorded history began with the Normans. Like most villages in French Flanders, it was caught up in the wars that bedevilled the region thereafter until Waterloo brought a lasting peace. Like them, too, it was, and still is, a farming village, its fields given over to maize, wheat, vegetables and cattle. In 1913 the population was 955, about the same as now. The layout is largely unchanged as well, despite the number of buildings increasing from 217 to almost 300. They are evenly distributed between the D22, which runs north-south through Fromelles, and the D141, on which it is flanked by le Maisnil and Aubers, 1.5 miles northeast and southwest respectively. The ridge on which all three stand takes its name from Aubers.

Actually to call it a ridge is to abuse the word. Stretching northeast from La Bassée for twenty miles to the west of Lille and nowhere more than 120 feet above sea level, it is more like a flattened speed bump on the ironing board flat plain that rolls northwards to Armentières. But the views this seemingly insignificant height commands in that direction are good. Traffic can be seen from it crawling along the D171, the arrow straight Rue du Bois/Tilleloy two miles away, and the church spires in the villages of Neuve Chapelle, Fauquissart, Fleurbaix and Laventie are beacons pointing skywards.

Prewar Fromelles. The view is south from the church tower. (M. Delebarre)

German observation post atop Aubers Ridge then...and now. (M. Delebarre)

The Battlefield

When stalemate settled on the Western Front at the end of 1914, Aubers Ridge lay within German territory. Apart from the observation it offered, the feature was also strategically important because it blocked the western approaches to Lille, the industrial centre of Flanders and a major rail junction, ten miles eastwards. As the loss of the ridge would be serious, the Germans dug a trench network on top, into which Fromelles and Aubers were incorporated, and deployed their artillery on the plateau behind. But they had no intention of making this system their front line because if it were, they would be fighting for the ridge itself at the start of any attack. Emphasising the basic defensive principle of depth, they gained the room necessary to secure their hold on it by pitching northwards onto the plain below.

Just over a mile from Fromelles, the German front line ran west across the Rue Delvas at N.9.d.4.1, now the Australian Memorial Park, before swinging sharply southwest at N.8.d. The resulting salient enfiladed No Man's Land, which was a massive 420 yards wide there. At its apex, a slight rise that may have been the site of an old farm building was called the Sugarloaf because its shape brought to mind the popular local bread. Continuing southwest, the line traversed the

14

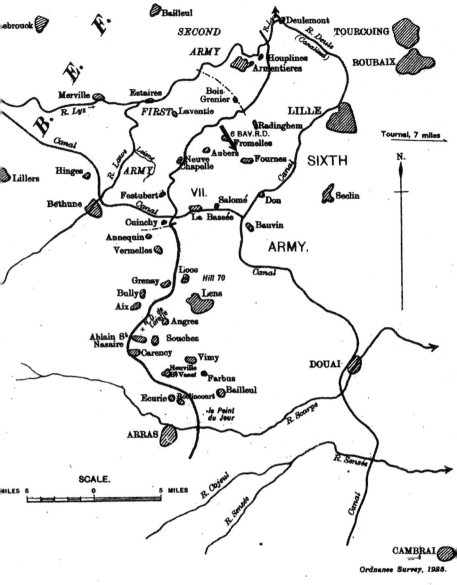

1. Fromelles within the Armentières-Lille area (Detail from *Official History – France and Belgium 1915*, Vol. 2, facing p. 3).

smaller Wick Salient at N.13.d.2.5 before crossing the Rue du Trivelet between Fauquissart and Aubers. In the opposite direction, another excrescence in N.11.a was called the Tadpole. Apart from the Sugarloaf area and a stretch 100 yards wide in N.10.c, the average width of No Man's Land was 250 yards.

The British line opposite was an archaeologist's delight. It headed southwest past the ruins of l'Abbaye Chartreux at Boutillerie hamlet in N.5.c to Cordonnerie Farm at N.10.a.8.4, whose buildings were ringed by a medieval moat. Swinging west at some crumpled mounds and a larger moat 300 yards further on, all that remained of another medieval farm, the line jumped the Rue Delvas at N.9.c.6.7 and then ran southwest in front of the Rue du Bois. This road was the artery on which the British in the Fromelles sector depended. Laventie, a billeting centre two miles north of it, was the setting for Eric Kennington's famous painting of 1/13 London Regiment, better known as the Kensingtons.

Scrubby grass had taken over the fields across which both front lines snaked, reinforcing the melancholy dreariness that so struck Lieutenant General Sir James Willcocks, commander of the Indian Corps:

> A dismal dead plain, dotted with farmhouses and here and there clumps of trees. The uninteresting roads metalled only in the centre; ditches and drains in every direction; observation beyond a very limited distance impossible, and for months the morning mists enveloped everything in a thick haze well into midday; canals, crossed here and there by bridges, added to the difficulties of communication . . . it was just a flat dreary expanse in winter and studded with green leaves and some wildflowers in summer.[1]

The flatness hindered British artillery registration by making the fall of shot hard to observe but the Germans, ensconced on Aubers Ridge, could see everything that went on below them. They were also dry there. On the plain, the water table sat a mere eighteen inches below the surface and flooding was the common enemy. Both sides went up

Flooded British breastwork at Laventie, winter 1914-15. Note burials at left.

rather than down, constructing breastworks of earth-filled sandbags, but were swamped all the same. During the winter of 1914/15 when the two lines were knee deep in water, the British and Germans alike occasionally stood outside the breastworks trying to keep warm. Ironically a maze of dykes, streams and ditches crisscrossing the area was supposed to keep the water at bay.

Many of these conduits drained into the Laies 'River', which had been dug to carry excess water to the Lys at Armentières. Six to ten feet wide, it ran behind the German line for 2.5 miles before exiting a stone's throw east of the Sugarloaf and then slicing obliquely through No Man's Land where VC Corner Cemetery stands today to enter the British line at N.9.c.7.7, near a small orchard. Its depth varied from three feet in summer to six feet during autumn and winter but if blocked by shelling, it became a real obstacle and the surrounding fields degenerated into muddy expanses. Even in dry weather, an attack across them might well have to pass over waterlogged ground. Buttressed by the all-seeing ridge, the understrength 13th and 14th Divisions of VII Corps were content to let the British do the attacking.

The Germans Strengthen Their Line

On 10 March 1915, General Sir Douglas Haig's First Army struck the salient at Neuve Chapelle, 1.5 miles southwest of Aubers, in the first British offensive of the war. As shell shortages limited the bombardment to thirty-five minutes, surprise was complete and Neuve Chapelle soon fell. But misunderstandings and delays in deploying reserves derailed the advance to the final objective, a line beyond Aubers that extended five miles across the ridge to the hamlet of Rouges Bancs below Fromelles. Haig called a halt four days and 13,000 casualties later.

Shocked at how easily Neuve Chapelle had been lost and aware that the ridge might have followed but for British mix-ups, the Germans acted quickly. After the 13th and 14th Divisions sideslipped westwards, the 6th Bavarian Reserve (BR) Division, which had been rushed from Lille during the battle, took over the 8,000 yards of line opposite the Fauquissart-Bois Grenier sector. It comprised 16 Bavarian Reserve Infantry Regiment (BRIR) – also known as the List Regiment after its shortlived first commander – and 17 BRIR from 12 BR Brigade and 20 and 21 BRIR from 14 BR Brigade. As three divisions now occupied an area previously held by two, the regimental fronts shrank from 3,000 to 2,000 yards, yielding the manpower needed to beef up the defences.

Overrun at the outset, the flimsy front line breastwork of piled sandbags, four feet high and five thick, was transformed right across the plain:

> The width of the parapet was doubled or even trebled to measure fifteen to twenty feet across and heightened to six or seven feet. It was then considered to be proof against the shell of all but the heaviest calibre armament on the British front. The wire entanglement, which in combination with the machine guns made the position so formidable, had been increased in breadth . . . Further wire had been erected in the excavations in front of the parapet - dug to obtain earth to build the parapet – which was not visible from the British trenches.[2]

Made with a heavier gauge, the new wire was as resistant to ordinary wire-cutters as it was to shrapnel. Assaulting troops had to throw greatcoats or blankets over the entanglements, which varied from six to fifteen yards deep, and clamber across them while under fire from machine guns emplaced in reinforced wooden boxes every twenty yards within the breastwork. Similar structures set every few yards sheltered two men each and sandbag covered dugouts (*Wohngraben*) immediately behind the breastwork gave additional protection.

The Germans also recognised the necessity of strong positions close behind the front line, which hitherto they had thought would only encourage timidity in its garrison. The support line, which existed only in outline 150-200 yards back, was refurbished and *Wohngraben* dug between it and the front line. In rear of the support line and arcing westwards before Fromelles and Aubers, Mouquet Farm at N.11.a.1.0, Delangré Farm at N.10.d.1.3, and Delaporte and Deleval Farms on the Rue Deleval at N.15.a.7.5 and N.14.d.5.4, were converted into strongpoints. Behind them and 700-1,000 yards from the front line, concrete pillboxes begun in February were to serve as rallying points while their machine guns swept the ground ahead in the event of a breakthrough. Whereas the communication trenches had been little more than surface scratches:

> There was now in every regimental sector an "Up" and a "Down" communication trench between the front position and some central point, a thousand yards or so in rear. These communication trenches had fire steps on both sides so that they could be used for defence, and in many places were hidden from view by means of canvas screens, or . . . covered by hurdles or other roofing, an arrangement that was to prove of considerable value in concealing the arrival of reinforcements and the carrying up of material.[3]

The First Battle

The new line was put to the test when the First Army attacked Aubers Ridge at 5.40 am on 9 May 1915. The main stroke south of Neuve Chapelle was supposed to link up with a secondary assault

The Battle of Aubers Ridge (*Official History – France and Belgium 1915, Vol. 2, facing p. 7).*

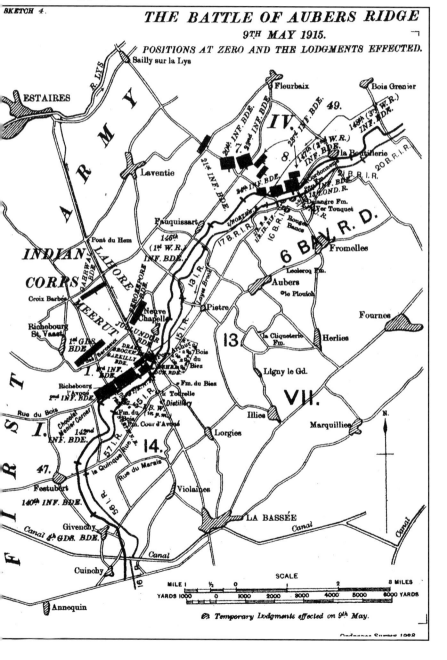

opposite Fromelles, where 2nd Lieutenant K.H.E. Moore of 1/7 Middlesex felt the tension as zero hour approached:

> *Sunday broke a glorious day with the corn and fields looking perfect. It was light about three but it was not until five that the show was to start. The first line trenches in which we were and the assembly trenches were by this time simply packed with troops and of course it seemed an eternity waiting for our watches to point to five o'clock. However, it came at last and to the very tick hundreds of guns started pounding away. . . The noise was terrific and the ground simply shook like a jelly.*[4]

Things went wrong from the start, and not only because the Germans had heightened their vigilance the day before. Owing to faulty ammunition and worn guns, duds landed everywhere and errant live shells, dubbed 'dropshorts', pounded the British line throughout the bombardment. Although the German line disappeared in a cloud of dust and smoke, it was largely undamaged and the garrison emerged at 5.25 am to man it. When the cloud briefly cleared, their bayonets were seen above the breastwork. Shouting out to the attackers that they had expected them twenty-four hours earlier, the Germans swept away the main assault south of Neuve Chapelle in twenty minutes.

Major General Richard Haking, who commanded the 1st Division, launched a second assault. It failed as disastrously as the first. Undaunted, Haking suggested making a third attempt after midday to his corps commander, Lieutenant General Sir Charles Monro. He was reluctant but Haig approved. Getting fresh troops through the congested communication trenches proved so difficult that it had to be postponed until 4 pm.

Meanwhile Major von Lüneschloss, who commanded 3/16 BRIR, watched from his headquarters in Fromelles as the 8th Division started the secondary attack. Separate assaults by 24 and 25 Brigades set out towards the village on a 1,400-yard frontage, with the main effort astride the Rue Delvas. Once again, the bombardment left large sections of the German line intact but rained dropshorts on the British one. The consequences were ghastly:

> *5.30 am over the top . . . My batman and I almost immediately blown up by our own barrage, 18 lb shell from behind, and crouched wounded in a shallow field ditch, soaked by blood and brains of a soldier who was apparently beheaded and lay over us – and probably protected us from further damage. When worst storm and carnage abated, I was found and carried back by stretcher-bearers . . . about 7 am. I heard no more of my batman.*[5]

20

On the right flank of 24 Brigade's attack west of the Rue Delvas, 2/Northamptonshires had to cross 330 yards of No Man's Land while fully exposed to the Sugarloaf. They were wiped out apart from thirty men who miraculously reached a gap smashed in the line by an eighteen-pounder manhandled into the British breastwork the night before, its wheels fitted with rubber car tyres to minimize the noise. Supporting them 300 yards closer to the road, 2/East Lancashires, and 1/Sherwood Foresters crumpled before devastating enfilade machine gun fire. German rifleman stood on the parapet to get a better shot at them.

Across the road, the bombardment had been more effective and No Man's Land was only 100 yards wide, giving 2/Rifle Brigade and 1/Royal Irish Rifles the edge they needed. The two battalions from 25 Brigade captured 250 yards of breastwork and a number of prisoners before storming another 300 yards to Rouges Bancs. But the Germans on the flanks recovered quickly and poured fire into 2/Lincolnshires, the supporting battalion, stopping them cold.

At Cordonnerie Farm on 25 Brigade's eastern flank, two mines had been dug under 3/16 BRIR's line. When they were blown from Cellar Farm at zero hour, two smoking craters remained where eighty yards of it had been. The Kensingtons seized both, but again the Germans on either side soon rallied and raked the companies following. Enough

Firing the mine from Cellar Farm before the Kensingtons go over, 9 May 1915.

2/Lincolns moving through German prisoners and the wounded of both sides in one of the craters. (M. Delebarre)

men survived to relieve those in the craters, whereupon they overran the strongpoint at Delangré Farm before forming a protective flank in a communication trench called the Kastenweg.

Following the battle from his headquarters in Fournes, two miles southeast of Fromelles, Brigadier General Kiefhaber, 16 BRIR's commander, ordered Lünenschloss to move 3/16 BRIR's headquarters to the Türkenecke strongpoint behind Delangré Farm at N.16.b.2.7, so that he could exercise closer control. In addition, Kiefenhaber put Major Arnold's 1/16 BRIR on alert in Fournes at 6.30 am. The neighbouring regiments, 17 and 21 BRIR, were already assisting and, perversely, the British tactics also helped. Thanks to the wide gaps

1/16 BRIR standing by at Fournes.

between the attacking battalions, the pockets secured were too far apart to support each other and the Germans between them were never threatened.

Machine-gunned from their flanks and rear, 2/Rifle Brigade and 1/Royal Irish at Rouge Bancs withdrew to the German front line, whereupon a bogus order started a retirement across No Man's Land. Mistaking the prisoners with the withdrawing troops for a counterattack, British machine gunners opened fire as well. Brigadier General A.W.S. Lowry Cole fell mortally wounded while standing on the parapet to rally his command. But the remainder of the Lincolns he had ordered forward gained another foothold in the German line, and some 2/Royal Berkshires reached the Kensingtons.

Still, the 8th Division's attack had stalled. Haig wanted it renewed without delay but conditions in the line and the communication trenches, both of which were full of wounded and men who had been driven back, meant otherwise. The assault was fixed for 1.30 pm. This time the British guns hit 1/Worcestershires and 1/5 Black Watch from 24 Brigade while they waited to go over the top, the German artillery pitched in as well and machine guns swept the parapet. The attack was aborted. 25 Brigade fared no better.

The 4 pm attack south of Neuve Chapelle would now have to go in unsupported against defences more strongly manned than they had been in the morning. Of the Black Watch from Haking's reserve brigade, fifty men reached the German support trench, only to be cut off after the following waves were mown down. The Camerons, Gloucesters and South Wales Borderers barely got past their own

The aftermath of the 4 pm attack. Cameron dead in front of the British parapet.

parapet. Haking ordered yet another assault as soon as they could be reorganised but backed down when his brigadiers protested that it would amount to a criminal undertaking. The heaviest machine gun fire of the day and a deluge of British dropshorts annihilated the attack of the neighbouring Meerut Divison from Willcocks's Indian Corps.

The end was also near for the men holding out below Fromelles, where Kiefhaber had sent 1/16 BRIR at 2 pm. By then, the eighty Kensingtons surrounded at Delangré Farm were all killed or captured and many others, both Kensingtons and Berkshires, had been driven back to the mine craters. Those still within the German line faced a dreadful withdrawal when the order to pull out was given at 2.45 pm:

> We crawled for hours above our waists in the mud and foul water of the German trenches, isolated and cut off by an enemy we could not see, but who was steadily reducing our numbers by very excellent sniping. We were four subalterns in command of thirty to forty men. Two of the officers were killed. The other man and myself determined to wait until darkness and then try to get through the German lines to our own. It was a risk, but everything was a risk that day.[6]

The surviving Northants withdrew at 8 pm. With no grenades left and fighting hand-to-hand, the Lincolnshires broke out shortly afterwards. 2/Rifle Brigade and 1/Royal Irish Rifles in the German front line held on until 3 am. A crucifix memorial to Lieutenant Paul Kennedy, who commanded B Company of 2/Rifle Brigade, and three of his brother officers, all of whom fell in this fighting, has stood on the Rue Delvas near Rouge Bancs since 1921.

Lieutenant Paul Kennedy.

Reports of heavy losses and low shell stocks arrived at Haig's headquarters early on the morning of 10 May. Acknowledging that the German defences were much stronger than anticipated and would need a lengthy bombardment for the assaulting infantry to have any chance of success, he cancelled a proposed further attack. In all, the fifteen hours of fighting cost his Army 11,619 men. Haking's division lost 3,968 but the 8th Division, with 4,682 casualties, paid the heaviest price. Opposing it below Fromelles, 16 BRIR lost 594 men of the German total of 1,551.[7] The front lines were unchanged.

Grave of Brigadier General A.W.S. Lowry Cole, Le Trou Aid Post Cemetery

Going For Concrete

Notwithstanding the artillery ammunition problems, the British Official History considered the main cause of the failure to be 'the strength of the German defences and the clever concealment of machine guns in them.'[8] From the German standpoint, the line had indeed stood up well overall. But some of the penetrations occurred where 6-inch howitzers had hit the breastwork, confirming fears about its susceptibility to heavy shells.

Concrete was the answer. Many of the machine gun posts in the breastwork were encased in it, effectively making the front line a string of pillboxes covered with sandbags and earth. In between them, concrete shelters equipped with sliding metal doors to defeat raiding parties replaced the wooden boxes. Subterranean emplacements were constructed a few hundred yards in rear for *minenwerfer*, the 24.5-cm trench

Minenwerfer **crater behind the Australian line at Cordonnerie Farm.**

Loading a 24.5 cm heavy *minenwerfer.*

Underground *minenwerfer* pit behind Delangré Farm excavated in 1995. The bomb that caused the damage in the previous picture was probably fired from it. (M. Delebarre)

mortar, whose 200-lb projectile left a crater the size of a house. One was excavated just behind Delangré Farm at N.10.d.2.1 in 1995. The farm strongpoints were strengthened and multi-roomed blockhouses, like the one built by *Bau-Pionier-Kompanie* 13 at N.16.c.1.1, reinforced the pillbox line behind them. On the ridge, 'Bayern Nord' blockhouse, complete with an observation level, became the forward headquarters of 16 BRIR at N.23.c.0.3. The interior of Fromelles church was turned into:

An intact concrete observation post amidst the rubble pile of Fromelles church. (M. Delebarre).

...a solid cube of concrete, except for a stair so narrow that only with difficulty could a normally built man ascend...It terminated in a loophole for an observer, who with a telescope could, with perfect safety to himself, count every sentry in our lines. He also had an extensive view across our back areas, and could at once detect any preparation for attack.[9]

The adjacent houses were similarly fortified, as were Aubers church and the houses around it.

Besides improving the defences, the 6th BR Division largely won its battle against the water table. The installation of electric pumps and a system of drainage sumps kept much of the line and the *Wohngraben* dry even in the winter of 1915-16, except on the left where 17 BRIR extended through the Wick Salient to the Rue du Trivelet south of Fauquissart. Blockages in the Laies forced it to abandon some parts of the line temporarily and reduce the garrison in others until conditions returned to normal in February 1916. In April, when more heavy rain brought three feet of water, they became wretched again.

Having been in the same sector for over a year by this time, the 6th BR Division knew it intimately. Next to 17 BRIR, 16 BRIR held the Sugarloaf. 21 BRIR began just west of the Rue Delvas and 20 BRIR stretched from the Tadpole eastwards. Whereas each regiment had originally put two battalions in the forward system, the strengthening of the line after May 1915 permitted a reduction to one and made the support trenches behind the breastworks redundant. Half of the second battalion manned the farm strongpoints and the blockhouses and earthworks 800 yards rearwards. Part of the other half occupied the line on the ridge, with the rest in Fromelles, Aubers and le Maisnil as regimental reserves. Further back in villages such as Fournes, the third battalion served as a brigade or divisional reserve. All reserve units practised counterattacks via the blockhouses and communication trenches.

As for its standing, the 6th BR Division was considered a trench formation rather than an élite division. C.E.W. Bean, the Australian Official Historian, described it as having been:

raised immediately after the outbreak of war from untrained men under or over military age, with a proportion of fully trained but elderly reservists.[10]

Nonetheless two years later, men such as twenty-seven year-old Lance Corporal Adolf Hitler, billeted at a butchery in Fournes as a runner in 16 BRIR, were veterans of First Ypres, Neuve Chapelle, Aubers Ridge and actions since. They had developed a position that

Adolf Hitler in Fournes. On the march (1) and with friends (seated right).

already favoured the defence into an obstacle of great depth and their tactics of holding the front line thinly but liberally providing it with machine guns, coupled with reserve battalions trained to counterattack swiftly from secure locations well back, had proven difficult to counter. Most important of all, their morale was excellent.

NOTES

1. J. Willcocks, *With the Indians in France* (Constable, 1920), p. 81.
2. J.E. Edmonds, *Military Operations: France and Belgium, 1915. II. Battles of Aubers Ridge, Festubert and Loos* (Macmillan, 1928), pp. 14-15.
3. *Military Operations: France and Belgium, 1915,* p. 15.
4. Quoted in A. Bristow, *A Serious Disappointment* (Pen and Sword, 1995), pp. 65, 85.
5. Quoted in Bristow, op. cit., pp. 86-7.
6. Capt. Kimber quoted in Bristow, op. cit., p. 121.
7. *Military Operations, 1915. II,* p. 39; Bristow, op. cit., p. 172.
8. *Military Operations, 1915. II,* p. 41.
9. Brig. Gen. H.E. Elliott quoted in R. McMullin, *Pompey Elliott* (Scribe, 2002), p. 508.
10. C.E.W. Bean, *The Official History of Australia in the War of 1914-1918. III. The AIF in France: 1916* (Angus & Robertson, 1942), p. 351. Hereafter OH.

Chapter Two

THE AUSTRALIANS AND THE BRITISH

For the British, Fromelles was part of the Fleurbaix sector, which took its name from the village a mile behind the line where many of them were billeted. As no major fighting occurred in the area after May 1915, they used it as a 'nursery' to introduce new formations to trench warfare. I Anzac Corps (ANZAC) went there on arriving from Egypt in April 1916. Its three divisions, the 1st and 2nd Australian and the New Zealand, held the nine-mile front from the Lys to opposite the Sugarloaf on the right of General Sir Hubert Plumer's Second Army.

Although the village *estaminets* and the worldly charms of nearby Armentières offered pleasures heretofore unknown, the Australians soon realised that the Western Front would be much tougher than Gallipoli and the German a more redoubtable adversary than the Turk. Steel helmets were a novelty and gas, flame-throwers and the omnipresence of aircraft all new. The sniping was deadly and shells fell suddenly, accurately and often. Several hundred men were lost before the Australians realised that the cause was not spies but their own carelessness as they hung out washing in full view of Aubers Ridge or stood about in the open watching aerial dogfights. Neither side gained the upper hand in the struggle to dominate No Man's Land.

On 5 May, a German raid on the Bridoux Salient, a mile east of la Boutillerie, captured two of the still secret Stokes mortars, embarrassing the AIF for a long time. When 21 BRIR raided Cordonnerie Farm on 30 May, the bombardment, to which the *minenwerfer* at Delangré Farm contributed tellingly, was the heaviest the Australians had known and caused most of their 116 casualties. The commander of the 2nd Division, Major General J.G. Legge, admitted that the initiative lay with the enemy, who was, 'so far as he can be without actually attacking, somewhat superior in the offensive'.[1]

I ANZAC itself carried out fourteen raids between 5 June and 2 July 1916, most of them in response to a directive Haig had issued on 28 May. Now the BEF's commander-in-chief, Haig called on his other armies to launch raids that would distract German attention from the Fourth Army's preparations for its offensive on the Somme and wear down divisions the Germans might send there after it began on 1 July. As part of the programme, 1 Battalion hit 20 BRIR east of Petillon on 28 June. Three nights later, 150 raiders from 9 Battalion inflicted seventy-nine casualties on 21 BRIR east of the Sugarloaf. The Germans lost over one hundred men when 11 Battalion raided the Tadpole on 2 July.

The nursery area was distinctly tense when I ANZAC, ordered to the Somme, handed it over to Lieutenant General Alexander Godley's newly arrived II ANZAC on 3 July. The 4th Australian Division entered the line alongside the New Zealanders, who had been transferred to Godley's corps, and the 5th Australian Division concentrated around Blaringhem, near Hazebrouck. On 8 July, the 4th Division, less its artillery, was ordered to follow the 1st and 2nd to the Somme and the 5th prepared to relieve it.

The 5th Australian Division

Consisting of 8, 14 and 15 Brigades, the 5th Division resulted from the AIF's expansion in early 1916. Sixteen new battalions were created by splitting the original sixteen, which had fought throughout the Gallipoli campaign, and drawing on the reinforcements assembled in Egypt to bring both halves up to strength. 1 Brigade from New South Wales provided the nucleus of 53, 54, 55 and 56 Battalions of 14 Brigade, the rest of which was made up of New South Welshmen. Victorians fleshed out 57, 58, 59 and 60 Battalions of 15 Brigade, whose parent was 2 Brigade from Victoria. Known as an all-states brigade because 29, 30, 31 and 32 Battalions represented every state in the Commonwealth, 8 Brigade had been raised in Australia and contained very few Gallipoli men.

Major General James Whiteside McCay, the 5th Division's commander, was a prewar politician who had been Defence Minister in 1904-5. Ambitious, clever and volatile, he was also a schoolmate and militia colleague of General Sir John Monash, Australia's greatest soldier. Unlike Monash, who could make imbeciles feel like intellectuals, McCay did not tolerate fools gladly and made them feel like imbeciles. He was also a strict disciplinarian and indifferent to danger, evoking at best grudging respect in those he led, but more often than not dislike or even loathing. A difficult subordinate as well, he never hesitated to tell his superiors where he thought they were going wrong.

Major General J.W. McCay.

After commanding a militia battalion and then the Australian Intelligence Corps, McCay had just been appointed Deputy Chief Censor when he was given

2 Brigade AIF in August 1914. His handling of it at Gallipoli reflected the extremes to which he was prone. During the attack at Krithia on 8 May, for example, he leapt onto the parapet against merciless fire to wave his men on, threatened some with his revolver and called others cowards. In July McCay aggravated a leg wound received at Krithia and returned to Australia as a hero. Made AIF Inspector-General, he supervised the training and readiness of the AIF's recruits until appointed to command the 5th Division in February 1916.

When McCay arrived in Egypt on 22 March, 14 and 15 Brigades were preparing for a three-day desert march to defensive positions on the Suez Canal. Although many men had just been inoculated, McCay made it a test in which they had to carry full kit, pack and ammunition – a load of 90 lbs – in the 100° heat. Enjoying cooler conditions, 15 Brigade arrived in reasonable order but 14 Brigade, which preceded it, disintegrated. Private Charles Johnston of 56 Battalion particularly remembered the second day:

> All along the route one could see the articles thrown out by the boys. Here a few cartridges, then a towel, a pair of pyjamas, trousers, oilsheet...some threw out a few sheets of paper to lighten the load. The boys lagged and lagged behind, hundreds needing the doctor's attention, and many fainting. Many begged and begged for water.

Of the 900 who started from 56 Battalion, Johnston was one of 38 to march into Moascar, the day's objective. Parched, delirious with sunstroke and sometimes naked, the rest staggered in during the night 'like the remnant of a broken army'.[2] On reaching the canal, each battalion was paraded to hear an insulting rebuke from McCay, who said all ranks shared in the debacle and declared 14 Brigade unfit for

B Company 60 Battalion about to commence the desert march, 29 March 1916. (M. Wood)

Colonel H. Pope.

Brigadier General E. Tivey.

operations. For weeks afterwards, the battalions marched in circles with full packs for two hours daily as punishment.

Colonel Harold Pope, who had led 16 Battalion in some of the heaviest fighting at Gallipoli, replaced Brigadier General G.G.H. Irving as commander of 14 Brigade. A giant with a personality to match, Brigadier General Harold Elliott of 15 Brigade had commanded 7 Battalion during the action at Lone Pine, for which it was awarded four Victoria Crosses. Commissioned into 2/Royal Berkshires during the Boer War, he chose to stay with his Australian unit instead and won the DCM. Brigadier General Edwin Tivey of 8 Brigade earned a DSO in South Africa but missed Gallipoli. His brigade was called Tivey's Chocs because it lacked nothing on leaving Australia.

Brigadier General Sydney Christian, another Boer War veteran and the only regular soldier amongst the 5th Division's senior officers, had perhaps the hardest job as its artillery commander. The higher artillery establishments of divisions on the Western Front necessitated quadrupling the Australian artillery, which meant that the 4th and 5th Divisions had to raise theirs practically from scratch. Of Christian's 3,000 men, fewer than 500 were trained gunners. The rest came from the newly formed infantry battalions and the light horse units. As the few guns available for training had to be used in relays, only elementary firing practices could be completed. Through no fault of its own, the artillery had not reached the necessary standard when the 5th Division left for France in June.

On 5 July, as the 5th's officers were visiting the line between Bois Grenier and the Sugarloaf that they were about to take over from the 4th Division, 13 Jäger Battalion, which had formed part of the Sugarloaf garrison, was identified on the Somme. Plumer had already sent II ANZAC another appeal from Haig to prevent such transfers and, on 7 July, Godley told McCay that 'that raids and all possible offensive (sic) should be undertaken at once'. McCay ordered Lieutenant Colonel Walter Cass, who had been wounded at Krithia and now commanded

Brigadier General H.E. Elliott.

54 Battalion, 'to do a raid tomorrow night'. When Cass protested that his men, like the rest of the 5th Division, had yet to see the front line and had little idea of how to undertake a raid, McCay retorted that 'it had got to be done and could be done all right'. Pope and Tivey also confronted McCay and Elliott may have joined them. McCay gave in.[3]

Lieutenant Colonel W.E.H. Cass.

The twenty-mile march forward began on 8 July and next evening the brigades were billeted in the villages from which they were to relieve the 4th Division. On 10/11 July, 29 and 30 Battalions left Erquinghem for 8 Brigade's sector in front of Bois Grenier on the left, while 57 and 58 Battalions from 15 Brigade, co-located with the divisional headquarters in Sailly, moved in opposite the eastern face of the Sugarloaf on the right. 14 Brigade filled the centre with 55 and 56 Battalions from Fleurbaix on 11/12 July. Each battalion held 1,000 yards of front and the 4th Division's artillery, deemed too inexperienced to go with it to the Somme, stayed behind in support.

Daylight brought the irresistible temptation to look over the sandbagged parapet across a wilderness of foot high summer grass and self-sown crops at the German line. 30 Battalion's history records how lively the nursery had become:

> ...it was not long before a man was shot in the forehead and the cry went up for stretcher bearers...machine gun fire went on almost continuously...Shrapnel had also to be contended with, and occasionally 5.9-inch shells played havoc with our parapets ... At night [No Man's Land] became a "fairyland" by reason of the sheaves of flares which each side sent up with a view to detecting raids or the activities of patrolling parties. We were obliged to admit that the enemy fireworks were superior to our own...thousands of large grey rats...played havoc with equipment, clothing and food.[4]

The 61st South Midland Division

At N.8.d.1.8, where Bond Street communication trench ran back to the Rue du Bois, forming the boundary between the First and Second Armies, the 61st Division took over. Assembled at Northampton in January 1915 from the home service men in the territorial units of the 48th Division, it had languished at the bottom of the pecking order as a second line territorial formation in a rapidly expanding British Army. Lacking arms and equipment, the division spent the year on home defence duties, which limited training. Towards the end of 1915, its best men were sent to reinforce the first line division in France and training had to start again. The 61st Division itself went to France at the end of May 1916, scarcely a month before the 5th Australian Division.

Major General Colin Mackenzie, the divisional commander, had fought in the Boer War and in colonial campaigns from India to the Sudan. Awarded the DSO in West Africa in 1900, Brigadier General Alistair Gordon led 182 Brigade, which consisted of 2/5, 2/6, 2/7 and 2/8 Royal Warwickshires. A burly Irish gunner, Brigadier General Cosmo Stewart, commanded 183 Brigade, which comprised 2/4 and 2/6 Gloucestershires and 2/6

Major General C.J. Mackenzie.
(M. Delebarre)

and 2/7 Worcestershires. He had received the DSO during the relief of Chitral in 1895. One-eyed Brigadier General Charles Carter commanded 184 Brigade. It was made up of 2/1 Buckinghamshire, 2/4 Oxfordshire and Buckinghamshire, 2/4 Royal Berkshire and 2/5 Gloucestershire, which had war poet Ivor Gurney in its ranks.

After the 61st Division relieved the 38th (Welsh) Division) early in June, Mackenzie's headquarters was in La Gorgue, just outside Laventie at L.35.b.8.9, and 184 Brigade on the left, 183 Brigade in the centre and 182 Brigade on the right held equal stretches of a line that began opposite the western face of the Sugarloaf, passed the Wick Salient and ended beyond Neuve Chapelle. 3 Australian Tunnelling Company mined along the frontage and the Welsh had dug Rhondda Sap, a water-filled trench 150 yards in front of the breastwork between N.8.c.6.5 and N.8.d.6.9, at the end of May to pinch out the apex of the re-entrant facing the Sugarloaf in the left sector.

Within a month, the 61st Division had launched eight raids, more than any of the neighbouring I ANZAC divisions carried out. The results were mixed and the cost high. German shelling savaged a raiding party from 2/4 Ox and Bucks just before it went over the top on 21 June and smashed a raid by 2/8 Warwicks five days later. 2/4 Glosters actually got into the German trenches on 4/5 July and 2/5 Warwicks attacked in daylight on 9 July. 2/4 Royal Berks had their turn on 13 July but the Bangalore torpedo party was hit on the way across and only the first wave of eleven men got through the German wire. At 5.50 am on 11 July, the Germans blew a mine in a tit-for-tat response to one the Australian tunnellers had exploded under them a week before. On 12 July a Stokes mortar fired without warning near D Company, 2/4 Ox and Bucks. Replying instantly, the Germans cleaned up an entire platoon.

The Rue Masselot. The houses in the distance are on the Rue Tilleloy, on the other side of which the British front line ran.

The reserve battalions got little rest, even though many of them were billeted in Laventie, which the German artillery left alone as long as the British did not shell Aubers. They supported the forward units with endless working parties. On 12 June, 182 Brigade supplied 268 men to the Australian tunnellers. 2/1 Bucks contributed 510 of the 2,500 men who carried 1,500 gas cylinders dumped on the Rue Masselot to the front line on 18 and 19 June. 2/6 Warwicks brought battle stores up on 6 July and helped the engineers after that. All things considered, the 61st Division got off to a rough start.

The Apostle of the Attack

XI Corps, the 61st Division's parent formation, was commanded by the man who had repeatedly hurled the 1st Division against the German line at Aubers Ridge a year earlier. Now Lieutenant General Sir Richard Haking, he had also fought in the Boer War and been wounded at Mons in 1914 while leading 5 Brigade. But he was best known for *Company Training*, published in 1913 and reprinted throughout the war. It exalted the offensive: 'There is one rule which can never be departed from and which alone will lead to success, and that is to push forward, always to attack'. Even an attack against a stronger force, Haking wrote, 'will win as sure as there is a sun in the heavens', and an aggressive spirit would overcome firepower and unfavourable ground. Joining the 1st Division just after Aubers Ridge, Robert Graves commented wryly: 'The last shows have not been suitable ones for company commanders to profit by his directions'.[5]

Lieutenant General Sir Richard Haking.

Haking's first battle as a corps commander was the ill-fated offensive at Loos in September 1915. He was supremely confident as he briefed the Guards division:

He compared the German line to the crust of a pie – one thrust and it would be broken and behind it he expected there would be so little resistance that they would have no trouble in carving a way through. But the Coldstream were old campaigners and the general perhaps noticed a look of scepticism on the faces of the men who had been out since Mons. He paused, then added earnestly, 'I don't tell you this to cheer you up. I tell you because I really believe it'.[6]

The two New Army divisions of XI Corps attacked first and lost 8,000 men out of the 10,000 who started out.

Haking's subordinates, like McCay's, found him difficult. Shortly after the 46th Division arrived in XI Corps, its senior staff officer, Lieutenant Colonel Philip Game, was calling Haking 'a vindictive bully'. In February 1916 Game, who would later become Governor of New South Wales, went further, describing him as 'really impossible, untruthful and a bully and not to be trusted'. Haking also had a fixation about Aubers Ridge. He was 'always very keen' to take the feature, remembered a brigade major in XI Corps, 'and always told us if we behaved ourselves we should be allowed to attack it'.[7]

On 29 June 1916, Haking applied his belief that a weak attacking force would prevail against a strong defending one by sending two Sussex Pals battalions from the 39th Division against the Boar's Head, a salient 2¼ miles southwest of the Sugarloaf. The bombardment barely dented the defences, on which the Germans, looking down on the preparations, had erected signs reading 'When are you coming over Tommy?' When the assault started, they called out 'Come on Sussex', while drenching them with machine gun and shellfire. The Sussex miraculously penetrated their line before being ejected with 1,153 casualties. Haking sacked Major General R. Dawson, the 39th Division's commander, but considered the operation a success that greatly improved its fighting value. Major Neville Lytton, who was present, viewed things differently:

> *...it seemed to us that there were others who were responsible, and, if they had lost their commands after this failure, possibly greater disasters may have been avoided, for a similar experiment was made a little later on with two divisions and the result was exactly the same. Naturally in the Communique our attack appeared as a successful raid.*[8]

The 'similar experiment' Lytton mentioned was the attack about to be made in front of Fromelles.

NOTES

1. 2 Brigade to Battalions, 17 May 1916, Item 213/1(2), AWM 25.
2. C.W. Johnston to his father, 31 March 1916, Author's Papers; OH, p. 291.
3. *OH*, p. 328; 'Historical Note. Fromelles', undated, Bean Papers, Item 243b, 3DRL/606, AWM.
4. H. Sloan, *The Purple and Gold. A History of the 30th Battalion* (Sydney, 1938), pp. 63-4.
5. R.C.B. Haking, *Company Training* (Hugh Rees, 1913), p. 103; T. Travers, *The Killing Ground* (Allen & Unwin, 1987), p. 48; R. Graves, *Goodbye To All That* (Penguin, 1976), p. 95.
6. L. MacDonald, *1915* (Headline, 1993), p. 493.
7. Game and E.C. Jepp quoted in McMullin, op. cit., pp. 205-6.
8. N. Lytton, *The Press and the General Staff* (Collins, 1920), p. 42.

Chapter Three

STUMBLING TOWARDS BATTLE

On 15 June 1916, Haking had suggested thirteen operations that XI Corps might undertake to support the Somme offensive. The Boar's Head attack was one of two that went beyond a raid. The second was for a still grander enterprise alongside the Australians:

> ...an attack with a view to capturing and holding permanently 2,100 yards of the enemy's trenches from the Fauquissart road at N.19.a.4.3 to the enemy's salient at N.8.d.5.3 [the Sugarloaf].[1]

General Sir Charles Monro.

But the plan gathered dust until 5 July when Haig, convinced that the Germans might be teetering on the Somme, ordered First and Second Armies each to select a front on which to break through in their sectors. General Plumer suggested the Sugarloaf, opposite the boundary between them, where the German line seemed thinly manned. Expanding upon Haking's earlier proposal, he recommended a joint operation to General Monro, who now commanded First Army, but warned him that he could only spare one division as I ANZAC was leaving for the Somme. On 8 July Monro told Haking to plan an attack in which XI Corps would be reinforced by a division from Second Army.

Next day, Haking outlined a scheme for an attack by three divisions on a 4,600-yard frontage against Aubers Ridge, 'to include the two main tactical localities on the ridge, the high ground around Fromelles and the village of Aubers'. A four-hour bombardment was to precede it, with feint shelling further south at Givenchy and Cuinchy to draw off the German artillery.[2] But Monro felt that a thrust from Loos held better prospects in the event of a Somme success. He turned Haking down.

The attack was not off for long. On 13 July, Haig was informed that eight German battalions had followed 13 Jäger to the Somme from the Lille area. As the raiding programme had failed to stop them, stronger action was necessary, especially with the second great attack on the Somme about to begin. Thinking that a threatened advance on Lille by the First and Second Armies might work, General Headquarters (GHQ) resurrected Haking's Aubers Ridge plan, but as an artillery demonstration with a few raids added. The two Armies could assemble

360 guns – six divisions' worth of artillery – astride their boundary for a three-day bombardment on a 15,000-yard front to make the Germans think a new offensive was contemplated. But an infantry advance was to be provided for in case an opportunity arose later on.

Haig's Deputy Chief of Staff, Major General Richard Butler, hurriedly visited Monro's headquarters at Chocques to tell him what was intended. Finding that Monro preferred Haking's plan to a purely artillery demonstration, Butler decided that the infantry advance should not be an optional extra. It was provisionally fixed for 17 July, with a division from Second Army augmenting the 31st (Pals) and 61st Divisions of XI Corps. Haking was the obvious commander. Next, Butler explained the arrangements to Plumer and Godley at II ANZAC headquarters at La-Motte-au-Bois. Plumer readily concurred and lent the 5th Australian Division to First Army for it.

Briefing Haking at 6.30 pm on 13 July, Monro stressed that the objective must be limited to the German front and support lines. Widening his original frontage, Haking opted to seize 6,000 yards of both between N.19.a.3.3 on the Rue du Trivelet and N.6.c.6.5 opposite la Boutillerie, virtually the entire sector held by the 6th BR Division. XI Corps would assault astride the Sugarloaf with the 61st Division on the right and the 31st Division extending to the Rue Delvas and the Australians on the left. Positions were to be taken up over the following two nights, when the additional artillery allocated would move in as well. The guns already in place were to start cutting the German wire next day and the feint shelling of Givenchy and Cuinchy would commence on 16 July.

At 11 pm on 13 July, McCay arrived at La-Motte-au-Bois to be told that his division was temporarily joining XI Corps for the attack. The New Zealand Division and 60 Brigade from the 20th Division would take over the left half of its sector so that the Australians could concentrate on the narrower assault frontage. But at 2 am on the 14th, Haking learned that instead of sending him the guns of three divisions, Second Army was providing only the incompletely trained artilleries of the 4th and 5th Australian Divisions. Worse still, the ammunition allocation was slashed by a third to 215,000 shells. He immediately scaled down the operation by excluding the 31st Division.

The Plan

At a conference at his headquarters at Hinges at 9.45 am on 14 July, Haking told McCay and Mackenzie that their divisions would assault either side of Bond Street on a 4,000-yard frontage. The 61st Division

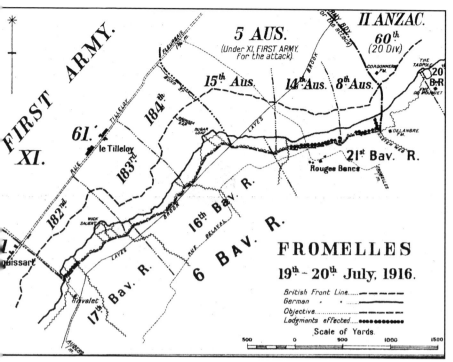

Map 3. XI Corps dispositions for the Fromelles attack.

on the right was to capture the 6th BR Division's front line from the Rue du Trivelet to where the Laies entered it, and the support line as far as the Laies. McCay's division on the left would capture the front line up to 'the track running north and south past FME DELANGRE (N.10.c.9.6)' and the support line as far as the Kastenweg. Reaching the support line, which British maps showed as the third and final trench of the maze behind the breastwork, involved a penetration of 150 yards. The Australians were also to seize the Delangré and Delaporte Farm strongpoints. Haking gave his commanders little latitude:

> [Each] *Division will attack with 3 Brigades in line, each brigade with 2 assaulting battalions, and each battalion on a front of assault of about 350 yards. The remaining battalions of the Division will be kept in Reserve and will not be used for assaulting the position without orders from G.O.C. XI Corps.*

The only exemption Haking allowed was the use of half a battalion from the reserve in each brigade as carriers behind the attack.

39

As for the artillery, the 8th Division's guns would support the 61st Division and 171 Howitzer Brigade from the 31st Division was allotted to the Australians. Wire-cutting would be continuous, and the heavy guns were to begin their registration and a slow bombardment on 16 July. A seven-hour bombardment before the assault on 17 July would start with more registration and wire-cutting and intensify over the last three hours, when four lifts to the barrage line shielding the advance were planned. Occurring at half-hourly intervals, they would last four, five, seven and ten minutes respectively. During each, the waiting infantry were to:

> ...*show their bayonets over the parapet; dummy heads and shoulders will be shown over the parapet, officers will whistle and shout orders, in order to induce the enemy to man his parapet. At the end of each of these lifts the artillery will shorten onto the enemy's front parapet and continue the intense bombardment of the front and support line.*

The feint bombardment would be fired on 16-17 July.[3]

This plan contained a major command and control error over the Sugarloaf Salient, one of the 61st Division's objectives but just a stone's throw from the inter-divisional boundary. Commanders regard boundaries as unfortunate necessities because the co-ordination measures operations across them require can easily break down. Hence they not should be sited on or near places critical to operational success, which the Sugarloaf certainly was. As the 'vital ground' for XI Corps, it had to be taken for Haking's attack to succeed.

At least four machine guns had been identified in the position. They

The Sugarloaf in the winter of 1919. The view is northeastwards in the direction of 15 Brigade's assault.

enfiladed both sides of the salient, where No Man's Land, 420 yards across, was at its widest. As the ground was so flat, they were also capable of grazing fire, in which the centre of each burst does not rise above the height of a standing man, for hundreds of yards along No Man's Land. This combination, enfilade grazing fire with a long dangerous zone, maximises a machine gun's lethality by enabling it to catch an assault flank on with no dead ground for cover. Because the Sugarloaf's machine guns could devastate both the Australian and British assaults in this way, the commanders on either side of the boundary near it had to be able to act instantly without compromising each other, not easy when they were out of touch in the heat of battle. Shifting the boundary so that only one formation was affected would have avoided the problem.

As in May 1915, everything depended on the artillery suppressing the German line until the infantry reached it. At 258, the number of field guns and howitzers was about the same as then and this time they were all modern. But they were also only as good as the men manning them and Haking well knew that many of the gunners were untried. Some of the heavy batteries were so new they had not fired a shot in France. Yet the heavies were the only means of knocking out the German guns and strongpoints, and hitting them demanded precise shooting.

The Division Commanders Get to Work

Of the twelve battalions in the 5th Australian Division, six had been in the front line for two days and the other six had not seen it all when McCay received his initial orders from Haking. The Australians would also be attacking over the same ground and against the same opponents as the 8th Division had. Nevertheless, McCay welcomed the attack. According to Bean, 'The fact that his division, though the last of the AIF to arrive in France, would be the first in serious action, gave [him] much gratification'.[4]

At Sailly on the afternoon of 14 July, McCay briefed his brigadiers. On the left, 8 Brigade was to assault between Cellar Farm Avenue at N.10.a.91/2.1 and N.10.c.1/2.6, and 14 Brigade in the centre from there to Pinney's Avenue at N.9.c.7.71/2. Each of these sectors was about 600 yards across but 15 Brigade's on the right stretched 900 yards to Bond Street. As the bend opposite the Sugarloaf meant that its right battalion would have to attack southeastwards to conform to the divisional boundary while the left one headed due south like 8 and 14 Brigades, McCay shifted Elliott's right 300 yards east to give both of his battalions a southerly assault. Four Vickers guns from 15 Machine

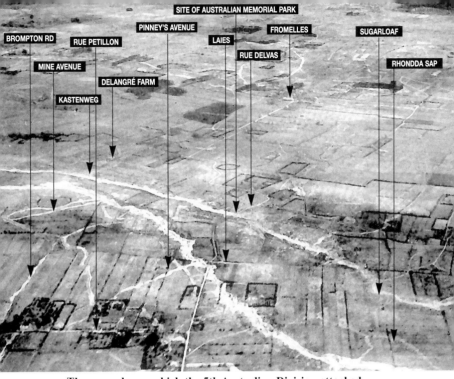

SITE OF AUSTRALIAN MEMORIAL PARK

PINNEY'S AVENUE

FROMELLES

SUGARLOAF

BROMPTON RD

RUE PETILLON

LAIES

RUE DELVAS

RHONDDA SAP

MINE AVENUE

DELANGRÉ FARM

KASTENWEG

The ground over which the 5th Australian Division attacked. (M. Delebarre)

Gun Company and five Lewis guns from 58 Battalion would fill the gap to Bond Street and protect 15 Brigade's flank by sweeping the Sugarloaf until the converging advance forced them to stop.

The two assault battalions in each brigade would attack in four waves one hundred yards apart, the first two waves starting from the breastwork. Behind them, the third and fourth waves were to form up in the 300 Yard Line, as the reserve line was known, with some platoons in the support line between it and the breastwork. These two waves would reach the breastwork just as the second wave set out after the first. When the fourth wave went over, the third battalions would be arriving from their assembly area on the Rue du Quesnes, which parallels the Rue de Bois 1½ miles rearward. Except for carrying parties, they were to garrison the front and 300 Yard Lines. By then the fourth battalions, which had assembled on the Rue du Quesnoy, another parallel road 1¼ miles further back, would have taken up positions on the Rue du Quesnes.

As the width of No Man's Land varied, McCay let the brigadiers decide when their first waves deployed into it to wait for the barrage to lift. The assault was on no account to go beyond the German forward system and each brigade had to dig two trenches across No Man's Land during the battle so that the captured line could be reached safely. As regards consolidation overall:

> The mode of taking the trenches should be as follows - first wave stays at and clears enemy out of first row of enemy trenches . . . Then advance further. Meanwhile second wave passes first wave to next enemy row . . and so on till all works of enemy first line system . . . are taken . . .
>
> It is the rearmost row of enemy's first line that is to be at once fortified and held when it is taken . . .
>
> Clearly understand that each wave, so soon as it has cleared of enemy the work it gets into, goes on to the prescribed limit of attack, ie the rearmost enemy work in his front line system, 100 yards to 150 yards behind his parapet.[5]

This 'conveyor belt' style of moving the waves forward would maintain the momentum of the assault and conformed to GHQ tactical notes. But they also warned that 'support points' must be established in rear to protect the men consolidating the new line, advice McCay ignored. GHQ further recommended that machine guns should be got up immediately. Deterred by the loss of the Stokes mortars in May, McCay directed that Lewis guns were to follow the last wave, while the Vickers guns and Stokes mortars would move only when 'it is fairly clear that we hold practically all [the position]'.[6]

Compared to the Australian brigades' average of 1,450 men on a 600-yard frontage, the three brigades of the 61st Division would each assault on a 750-yard frontage with 1,130 men. The explanation has always been that the 61st was understrength but recent analysis of its unit war diaries suggests otherwise.[7] Whatever the reason, its brigades would be attacking on a wider frontage than the Australians with fewer men. On the right, 182 Brigade was to go over between the Rue du Trivelet and N.13.Central opposite the Wick Salient, 183 Brigade in the centre from there to Sutherland Avenue, and 184 Brigade stretching to Bond Street on the left. Once in No Man's Land, the four waves were to lie down fifty yards apart with the leading wave eighty yards from

The attack frontage of the 61st Division as seen from Bond Street.

AUBERS

61 DIVISION

the German parapet. 'Directly the bombardment lifts, all four waves will advance at a walk, rushing forward if fired on'.[8]

In accordance with a direction from Haking, the British infantry would emerge from sally ports in the breastwork. The Australians ignored the order because they had found the method wanting at Gallipoli. Worried that his brigade could be left hanging if 184 Brigade was unable to clear the breastwork quickly, Elliott warned Carter that 'a single man getting shot in the sally port would spoil the whole attack.' Carter replied that 'he was going to try that way anyhow and if it failed he would send the men over the top'. Elliott commented, 'such a plan was bound to fail – you cannot rearrange your plans in a moment'.[9]

Tired Men

The overall plan was unravelling under the pressures of trying to mount a corps attack with two inexperienced divisions on three days' notice. Some batteries from the 5th Division had yet to reach the area, some from the 4th Division were rushing back to it after the cancellation of orders relieving them, and 171 Howitzer Brigade from the 31st Division and the British and Canadian medium trench mortar batteries, which replaced the raw Australian ones, were strangers to Brigadier General Christian. He was unable to deploy the bulk of his disparate units until 15 July. They started registration and wirecutting next day, a day late. A few 4th Division batteries were not in position until after the bombardment was supposed to have started on 17 July. Nonetheless, Haking's order, read to all ranks on the 16th, assured them that at the end of it, the artillery would have:

> Cut all the wire, destroyed all the enemy's machine-gun emplacements, knocked down most of his parapets, killed a large proportion of the enemy, and thoroughly frightened the remainder.[10]

Although wagons dumped the artillery ammunition near the battery positions, the infantry and engineers had to manhandle their ammunition and stores from the rearward dumps to the front line. Major Geoffrey Christie-Miller, 2/1 Bucks second-in-command, described what this entailed:

> Suffice it to say that some hundreds of preserved rations and tins of water, thousands of Mills Bombs, wire and piquets in profusion, and last but not least, an abundance of trench mortar ammunition, heavy, medium and light, if prepared on such a scale can provide a respectable

Major Geoffrey Christie-Miller.

*carrying load for a couple of Battalions for a couple of nights.
In addition, extensive revetting arrangements for the
consolidation of captured positions were made, and endless*
[Trench Mortar] *emplacements built.*[11]

During the afternoon of 15 July, gas was mistakenly
released from 2/7 Warwicks' line, causing several
friendly casualties. An hour-long discharge at 9 pm was
more successful. Ex-Cambridge first class honours
student Captain Geoffrey Donaldson got C Company out
of its dugouts and into gas helmets:

*There were words of command along the line from
the* [Royal Engineers] *and then a loud hissing sound
as the taps were turned on and the deadly greenish
white vapour poured out of the jets and slowly blew in
a great rolling cloud towards the opposite line of
trenches.*[12]

Captain Geoffrey
Donaldson.

17 BRIR lost twenty-five men. At 9.15 pm the German retaliatory
bombardment began to fall on A and B Companies of 58 Battalion,
which were about to hand over their line to 6/Oxfordshire from 60
Brigade so that they could shuffle onto their assault frontage. Cellar
Farm and Mine Avenues and the defences between them were
pulverised. As the shelling reached a crescendo at 11 pm, 1/21 BRIR
showed up. Lieutenant Härder led ninety-six raiders into the shattered
line, capturing a Lewis gun team after a sharp bomb fight. 58 Battalion
lost another 42 killed and 118 wounded and 6/Oxfordshire suffered 29
casualties. The Australians praised the raid as 'well staged'.[13]

On the afternoon of 16 July, the British assault battalions began
entering the line, some of them with incredibly little warning. 183
Brigade told 2/4 Glosters at 2 pm that they had to be in position by 6
pm for an attack early next morning, even though they were dispersed
between posts around Picantin and billets in Laventie. By feverish
effort, the scattered companies had concentrated at 7 pm, only to find
the ammunition dumps partly filled. They spent the night replenishing
them. 2/6 Warwicks received 'sudden' orders from 182 Brigade to
move up and then, about 9 pm, to prepare for an attack on the Wick
Salient. Once again, insufficient ammunition had been sent forward, so
carrying parties toiled through the night. Donaldson's company was
'very fatigued' afterwards. He himself had 'no time to reconnoitre the
ground of our advance'.[14]

The Australian brigades moved out on the evening of 16 July, many
men suspecting the soundness of the rushed preparations. Only those

in the first two waves had been issued with steel helmets. The rest would fight in their felt slouch hats. Apart from the bombing sections, no-one had been trained to use the Mills grenade. Engineers were still working on Brompton Road, 14 Brigade's lifeline, which was filled with water for three quarters of its length. Having to squeeze past them made the last part of the journey nightmarish.

Unless they had to go out on patrols to check the German wire or cut gaps in their own, most of the men in the assault battalions simply fell asleep on reaching the front line. When McCay rebuked 14 Brigade for failing to send a patrol out despite being ordered to do so, Pope replied that it had been unable to occupy any part of its front trenches until near daybreak. McCay remarked later on how noticeably fatigued the successive night movements and the heavy carrying work had left the Australians. The British battalions were described as 'tired but cheerful'. Fate intervened to lift the spirits of both.

Divided Generals

On 14 July, Major H.C.L. Howard, the staff officer who accompanied Butler when he called on Monro and Plumer the day before, had returned to confirm the arrangements with their chiefs of staff. As they declared themselves happy, Howard was surprised when Elliott showed him the Sugarloaf, 420 yards away across totally exposed ground, and said that, according to GHQ's own guidelines, 15 Brigade's attack had no hope. Venturing that he had only been at the front for a few days, Elliott asked Howard 'to tell me as man to man what he thought of it. He was much affected. He said, "Well, if you put it to me that way, I must tell you that it will be a bloody holocaust"'. Howard promised to tell Haig what he had seen.[15]

Lieutenant General William Birdwood, I ANZAC'S commander, and Brigadier General Cyril Brudenell White, its chief of staff, had expressed their reservations to GHQ at the outset. They thought the Germans would have to be dunces to treat an attack by two divisions with no reserves seriously. As for Haig's staff, the Boar's Head had reminded them how operations like the one now proposed had foundered in 1915. They were especially worried about the adequacy of the bombardment. So were staff officers in the 61st Division. Captain Philip Landon, 182 Brigade's staff captain, considered it 'ludicrously inadequate' for dealing with targets like concrete emplacements. One of his colleagues thought the artillery as a whole was 'hopelessly insufficient...both in numbers and training'.[16]

Noting these concerns, Haig approved the attack on 15 July but said the infantry should not go in unless the artillery was strong enough to take on the German guns. He sent Butler back to Choques with a stronger message next day. Meeting Plumer, Monro and Haking, Butler told them that Haig did not want the infantry to assault at all unless they were satisfied that they had enough artillery and ammunition not just to capture the position but to retain it. Then Butler dropped a bombshell. As the latest intelligence on the transfer of German reserves removed the urgent need to attack on 17 July, he asked whether the operation should be postponed or even cancelled.

Haking resisted vigorously. He assured Butler that the artillery was sufficient to get the infantry onto their objectives and keep them there, warned that postponing the operation would damage morale and said he was 'very confident of success'. Monro backed Haking and the pair told Butler that the attack should proceed, whereupon Haking asked whether he could carry on to Aubers Ridge if it went well. Butler came down hard, telling him that Haig wanted it to be strictly limited, 'however inviting' a further advance might be. When heavy rain fell during the afternoon, Butler returned to Choques to check its effect on the artillery preparation. As Monro was absent, he impressed upon his operations chief that Monro had full authority to postpone or cancel the attack because of the weather or any other reason.[17]

Then Haking put Monro on the spot. At 3 pm he had set zero hour, when the bombardment would start, for 4 am next morning, even though thick mists had hampered the artillery registration and wirecutting for the past two days. At 11 pm, after the rain had made things worse for the gunners, he postponed it to 8 am. Arriving in

Sailly-sur-la-Lys, headquarters of Generals Haking and McCay.

drizzle-laced fog at his advanced headquarters at Sailly at 6 am on 17 July, he deferred the start until 11 am. At 8.30 am, with the weather showing no sign of improving, Haking sought, with 'extreme reluctance', a postponement from Monro in a letter that acknowledged the awkward facts glossed over in his blustery performance with Butler. Not only was the heavy artillery brand new:

> *The infantry and field artillery...are not fully trained, and GHQ, from what was said at your conference yesterday, do not appear very anxious for the attack to be delivered... I should be glad to know if you wish me to carry it out tomorrow on the same programme.*[18]

Authorised to postpone or cancel the operation, Monro tried to do both. Agreeing to Haking's request, but fearing that the weather might force further postponements, he told GHQ at 10 am that he proposed to cancel the attack altogether. Because the Germans seemed about to counterattack on the Somme, making a holding action urgent again, GHQ replied that Haig wanted it carried out as soon as possible, weather permitting, so long as Monro was satisfied his resources were adequate. As he and Haking had already insisted they were and Monro felt reluctant, in the face of GHQ's pressure, to use the weather as an excuse, the attack was now as inevitable as the *Titanic* sinking after it struck the iceberg. At 7.15 pm on 17 July, Haking ordered it for the 19th, with the bombardment starting no earlier than 11 am and the infantry assaulting seven hours later.

The Hour Approacheth

Haking need not have worried about a postponement damaging morale. The worn out infantry, who had spent 17 July waiting to attack, were greatly relieved. Most of the assault battalions in the 61st Division withdrew to billets in Laventie, and Riez Bailleul a mile and a half southwest of it. The reserve battalions and one assault battalion from each Australian brigade returned to the brigade billetting area, Fleurbaix and Bac St. Maur for 8 and 14 Brigades and Sailly and Rouge de Bout for the 15th. Half of the other assault battalion went back to the 300 Yard Line, leaving the remaining half to garrison the breastwork. Elliott swapped his assault units, replacing 57 Battalion and the battered 58 Battalion with 59 and 60 Battalions.

Meanwhile, the Germans were retaliating for the artillery's stepped up registration and wirecutting. They pounded the Australian communication trenches, necessitating a continuous effort to keep them open. The parapet about N.8.b.7.0., where Elliott's machine gun company would occupy the gap between the two divisions, had to be rebuilt. Then an unidentified Australian battery began lobbing shells onto 2/1 Bucks' line. At 10 am on 18 July, one struck two of the gas cylinders hauled up five weeks earlier, causing 78 gas casualties in A Company. An order to take the cylinders back to the Rue Masselot dump arrived at 5 pm but 670 still remained next morning because 'The men were completely exhausted and nothing more could be done'.[19]

Final orders on the afternoon of 18 July emphasised the need for rest. McCay told his commanders to make certain their men had a good breakfast and midday meal before the attack next day. To ensure punctuality, he wanted the assault battalions assembled in the breastwork and 300 Yard Line by 3 pm, three hours before they were due to go over, and the reserve battalions on the Rue de Quesnes and Rue du Quesnoy by 5 pm. Late that night, he arranged with the Controller of Mines, Second Army, for a dormant mine to be fired at the moment of assault in No Man's Land at N.10.d.1.8, the area of the two mines blown during the 8th Division's attack in May 1915. The upturned edges of the crater would hopefully screen 8 Brigade's open flank from the Tadpole and Mouquet Farm.

As the last hours ticked away, many men wrote to loved ones, 'just in case'. Major Geoffrey McCrae, the 26-year-old architectural student whom Elliott had obtained from his old battalion to command 60 Battalion, penned a typically elegant letter to the well-known literary and artistic family from whence he came:

> Today I lead my Battalion in an assault on the German lines and I pray God that I may come through alright and bring honour to our name. If not I will at least have laid down my life for you and my country, which is the greatest privilege one can ask for. Farewell dear people, the hour approacheth.

Major Geoffrey McCrae.

Captain Waldo Zander of 30 Battalion felt a sense of anticipation: 'A stunt! We knew little what it meant, but to us it seemed something wonderfully new and exciting – a chance for a fellow to win his laurels and make good'.[20]

The Germans were more than ready to accommodate Zander for they knew exactly what was coming. As the preparations could only be completed by carrying them on in daylight, their observers on Aubers Ridge and in balloons above it saw the roads behind the British line clogged with men, vehicles and horses. The increased bombardment from 17 July and carrying parties seen on the 18th with what were assumed to be boxes of grenades and mats to throw over wire entanglements, confirmed that an attack was imminent. Villagers in Laventie, La Gorgue and other billets openly talked about an operation set for 19 July, and told 2/4 Glosters before their own orders arrived.

A light mist that morning heralded a perfect summer's day. The 6th BR Division had already alerted the two battalions in divisional reserve and at 7.15 am one of them, 1/20 BRIR, moved to Fournes. At 1 pm the line on the ridge stood to. Carrying parties were waiting to take grenades to the forward system. A sign above it asked 'Why so long, you are twenty four hours late?' The previous one had been shot away by the resentful recipients. It challenged them, 'ADVANCE AUSTRALIA - IF YOU CAN!'[21]

NOTES

1. Quoted in *OH*, p.259.
2. C. Wray, *Sir James Whiteside McCay* (Oxford, 2002), p. 178.
3. XI Corps Order 57, 15 July 1916, Item 1/22, Roll 774, AWM 4.
4. *OH*, p. 335.
5. 'Instructions for Brigadiers', 15 July 1916 and Order 31, 16 July 1916, 5 Aust Div War Diary (WD), July 1916, Item 1/50, Roll 836, AWM 4.
6. GHQ SS.109, 'Training of Divisions for Offensive Action', 8 May 1916, Monash Collection, 3DRL/2316, AWM; GHQ OB/1629, 4 May 1916, AWRS 359/10, AWM.
7. R.S. Corfield, *Don't Forget Me, Cobber* (Corfield & Co., 2000), pp. 69-73, 117-8.
8. 61 Div Order 28, 16 July 1916, Item 23/1, AWM 26; 184 Bde Order 16 and Instructions, 16 July, Item 27/1, AWM 26; 182 Bde Order 23, 16 July 1916, WO 95/3054, PRO.
9. H.E. Elliott, 'Private Memoranda on Supercession', 25 May 1918, Elliott Papers, 2DRL/0513, AWM.
10. *OH*, p. 339.
11. Memoirs of Colonel Sir Geoffrey Christie-Miller (unpublished, held by the Ox and Bucks Light Infantry Museum), p. 177.
12. Quoted in M. Brown, *The Imperial War Museum Book of the Western Front* (Motorbooks, 1994), p. 117.
13. A.D. Ellis, *The Story of the Fifth Australian Division* (Hodder and Stoughton, 1920), p. 87.
14. Entry for 17 July 1916, 2/6 Warwicks War D, WO95/3056, PRO; Brown, op. cit., p. 116.
15. Elliott, 'Private Memoranda'.
16. Quoted in McMullin, op. cit., p. 209.
17. OH, pp. 347-8; W. Miles, *Military Operations: France and Belgium, 1916. II. 2nd July 1916 to the End of the Battles of the Somme* (Macmillan, 1938), pp. 124-5.
18. Haking to 1st Army, 17 July 1916, Item 1/22, Roll 774, AWM 4.
19. R.B. Crosse, 'The Regiment in War XXXIII'. *Oxf & Bucks Lt Infantry Journal*, Vol. XII/67, May 1936, p. 77; 61 Div 'Report on Operations, 15-19 July 1916', 22 July 1916, Item 23/1, AWM 26.
20. McCrae to family, 19 July 1916, 12/11/104, 1DRL/0427, AWM; W.H. Zander, 'Narrative of Experiences', L/12/11/2737, 2DRL/0171, AWM.
21. L. Macdonald, *Somme* (Michael Joseph, 1983), p. 170.

Chapter Four

THE ATTACK OF THE 61ST DIVISION

In the early hours of 19 July, patrols from the 61st Division reported the line opposite as weakly held. The German artillery was quiet until the British and Australian shelling increased in the afternoon, whereupon the guns of the 50th (Reserve) and 54th Divisions joined the 6th BR Division's counter-bombardment. It battered the houses used by the British artillery observers on the Rue Tilleloy, worked over the batteries in the fields behind them, and blew up several ammunition dumps. Gunner losses were severe. But the waiting infantry were in high spirits. Their headquarters must have been impressed when they were asked just before the attack for a return on the number of pickle jars returned to store during the previous month.[1]

182 Brigade
The German shelling barely touched 182 Brigade's line, which 2/7 Warwicks held between the Rue du Trivelet and N.13.c.4.3$^{1}/_{2}$ on the right and 2/6 Warwicks from there to N.13.c.8$^{1}/_{2}$.8 opposite the Wick Salient on the left. At 5.30 pm Donaldson's C Company and D Company under Captain Thomas Bethell filed through two sally ports in 2/7 Warwicks' breastwork and into the shallow 'borrow-pit' in front without being fired upon. Forming up in their four waves, they started towards 3/17 BRIR's line, 250 yards ahead, at 5.50 pm, followed by 2 Section of 182 Machine Gun Company, while B Company moved into the ditch to support them.

When the barrage lifted at 6 pm, the two companies were fifty yards from the German parapet. They rushed it, entering on a 200-yard frontage between N.19.a.3.5 and N.19.a.6.8, where the breastwork and wire were completely destroyed. The front line was full of dead, and about one hundred Germans were captured as they emerged from their dugouts. Sent back across No Man's Land, half were killed when British machine gunners and artillery observers mistook them for a counter attack and opened fire.

As the bombers started along the breastwork towards the ditch at N.19.a.6.9 that was the boundary with 2/6 Warwicks, the attacking waves raced to the support line, dropping off men to form a protective block facing the Rue du Trivelet on the way. They arrived to find the wire intact. At that moment the machine guns of 10 Company 3/17

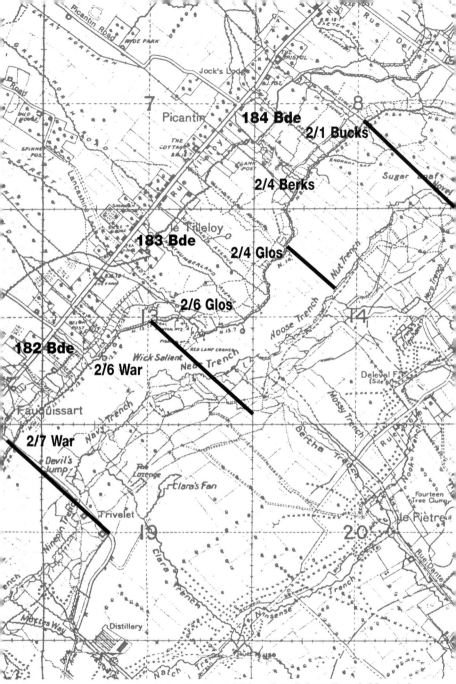

Map 4. The attack by the 61st Division (Detail from Trench Map Aubers, Sheet 36 SW1, Edition 10A, 1 January 1918).

German machine gunners in action. Many fired from the shelter of concrete emplacements.

BRIR, located west of the road, caught them in enfilade. Two Stokes mortars had been emplaced on that side at M.24.b.7.7 and M.24.b.6.4 to deal with these guns but were unable to locate them. Nor could the block do anything. The attackers were decimated. Frantically hacking through the wire, the remnants got into the shallow trench beyond at 6.10 pm.

The same machine guns flayed B Company and 2 Section as they reached the breastwork, which the German artillery had also started shelling. Casualties were crippling – only two of 2 Section's Vickers guns got into action. At 6.31 pm Lieutenant Colonel Herbert Nutt, the commanding officer, knew that his men in the captured line were alone and in trouble. A runner had arrived with a copy of a message sent back by 2/6 Warwicks: 'The 7th are across; our men won't face it. Send reinforcements'.

Commanded by Captains William Simms and Aubrey Coulton, A and C Companies of 2/6 Warwicks had emerged

Lieutenant Colonel Herbert Nutt.

53

3/17 BRIR's view from the Wick salient of the ground over which 2/6 Warwicks attacked.

from their sally ports at 5.31 pm. German shellfire mauled the left flank, where all the officers were casualties. The leading wave was eighty yards from 3/17 BRIR's parapet when the British barrage lifted. Just then another German deluge fell on No Man's Land and 'at the same time the German trenches became active with men and a large number of machine guns opened a heavy fire...mowing down the advancing lines'.

Although the Wick Salient was one of the most heavily bombarded parts of the German line, Lieutenant Reichenhardt and 11 Company were unscathed in their concrete shelters. When the shelling stopped, they raced for the parapet with three machine guns and shouted greetings to the Warwicks, who were still fifty yards away. The 182 Brigade account states that the machine guns were 'handled with the greatest bravery'. Riflemen and bombers also tore into the attackers. With a bag of grenades over his shoulder, Simms fell encouraging his men. Coulton was also killed. Following 100 yards behind, Captain Thomas Wathes led B Company over the dead and wounded. He was shot in the head and his men riddled.

In all, the equivalent of two platoons managed to reach the breastwork and the few who entered it were quickly overwhelmed. 2/6 Warwick's second objective, the support line between N.13.d.2.1 and N.13.d.5.2, was untouched. Lieutenant Colonel J.J. Shannessy sent D Company, in reserve on the Rue Masselot near his

Grave of Captain William Simms, Aubers Ridge British Cemetery. (J. Follet)

headquarters in the Apple House at M.18.b.4.4, to the front line but for the moment his attack was over. It had cost 238 casualties.[2]

The repulse of 2/6 Warwicks left the 2/7th isolated. At 6.37 pm Nutt ordered the digging of a communication trench to them but the intense German shelling of No Man's Land precluded it. A runner finally got through at 7 pm with a grim message sent by Donaldson forty-five minutes earlier: 'About twenty men hold enemy support line, it is being shelled'. Shortly afterwards, Major Welch in the forward signalling post saw the bombers, who had miraculously fought their way to the boundary with 2/6 Warwicks, being driven back by 'picklehaubes' moving down from the Wick Salient, and other Germans closing in from the Rue du Trivelet.

Nutt warned A Company, in reserve at the junction of the 300 Yard Line and Masselot Street communication trench, to be prepared to reinforce the captured line or meet a counterattack. Commanding from Cockshy House at M.4.c.1.1 in Laventie, Brigadier General Gordon rushed forward the brigade reserve, B and C Companies 2/8 Warwicks under Captain Tracey Lefroy, which were also in the village. 1 Section of 182 Machine Gun Company, which Gordon was holding at Masselot Post, also hurried up after receiving an erroneous message that the Germans had broken through.[3]

3/17 BRIR's counterattacks had begun almost as soon as its line was breached. Sergeant Lachenmayr formed two grenade teams from the survivors in the breastwork to take on 2/7 Warwicks' bombers. No sooner had Donaldson's men reached the support line than Lieutenant Schattenman sealed off their left flank with 9 Company, while 10 Company's machine guns pinned down the right. Unable to contact regimental headquarters, Captain Petri, 3/17 BRIR's commander, ordered part of 4 Company 1/17 BRIR to assault from the strongpoint it was holding behind the support line and summoned 1 Company, 17 BRIR's reserve, from Aubers. Sergeant Herb's platoon was the first to arrive and Petri sent it to reinforce Lachenmayr. When the second platoon joined them, the 'picklehaubes' were strong enough to drive the Warwick bombers back. The third platoon helped Schattenman.

Lieutenant Lutterloh, 4 Company's commander, had only forty-two men. He sent some against the block on his left and led the rest across the open against the apex of Donaldson's position. They stormed over it and towards the breastwork, where a shower of Mills bombs momentarily checked them thirty-five yards short. Cheering, Lutterloh's group charged and soon met Schattenman and Herb. At 7.45 pm the entire position had been retaken and the Germans turned two of the four Vickers guns lost by 2 Section against the British line. 2/7 Warwicks lost 383 men. Donaldson and Bethell were among the dead.

183 Brigade

No Man's Land in front of 183 Brigade was 200 yards across and at one point 150 yards, making it the narrowest stretch along the 61st Division's line. The engineers had driven exits under the breastwork so that the assault waves could move unseen into the 'borrow pit'. Two 'pipe pushers', ammonal-filled pipes pushed out into No Man's Land a few feet below the surface, had been blown at 4.30 pm to provide ready-made communication trenches. Because 3/16 BRIR opposite also held the line facing 184 Brigade and much of 15 Australian Brigade, 183 Brigade's attack would fall mainly on a single company, the 9th, commanded by 2nd Lieutenant Reher. For all these reasons, it was better placed than either of its sister brigades.

Unfortunately, the German bombardment hit 183 Brigade hard and forced both assault battalions to draw on their reserve companies to replace losses. Conversely, the British bombardment did little damage to the German breastwork and the wire was virtually uncut. Captain Gebhardt, the commander of 3/16 BRIR's front line, had ordered its lookouts to remain at their posts throughout the shelling so that the moment of the assault would not be missed. They saw the leading waves start through the sally ports. Haking's order to use them left idle

A pipe pusher sap.

the underground exits that would have concealed 183 Brigade's forming up.

The after action report of Lieutenant Colonel J.A. Tupman, commanding officer of 2/4 Glosters, the left assault battalion, left nothing to the imagination:

> At 5.31 pm, the time ordered for deployment in NO MAN'S LAND, A Coy (the left assault) filed out through Sap 7a and successfully deployed three platoons...D Coy (the right assault) was delayed for a few minutes, and by 5.50 pm had its leading platoon deployed in NO MAN'S LAND, the next platoon of this forming the 2nd wave partly out. At this point in the operations a heavy machine gun fire was opened on D Coy in the open, and the men were driven back on me into the Sally Port of sap 9 where I was standing. This machine gun fire was particularly heavy and appeared to come from the Front and Right Front from at least 5 or 6 M.Gs.
>
> At 5.55 pm I received a report saying A Coy was pushing on all right and I at once ordered the 2nd, 3rd & 4th waves of D Coy to be moved to the other Sally Port (No. 7a), and gave the Officers orders to push out there as rapidly as possible and to work up to the right of A Coy. I then went to the Sally Port (7a) and on arriving there found that A Coy by that time 6.10 pm had also been driven back. I ordered that the men should be collected and all be ready for a push forward should the opportunity occur. At the time I considered further attempt to advance in the face of this M.G. fire useless.[4]

Lieutenant James Digby Wyatt called the attack 'more a massacre than a battle'.[5] Both company commanders numbered among the 163 casualties. Captain E.H. Woodward of A Company was wounded but D Company's Captain Richard Byers fell. Tupman was evacuated sick next day.

When the first wave of 2/6 Glosters on the right entered the sally ports at 5.40 pm, Reher's men were fully alert as 2/4 Glosters had gone out nine minutes earlier. They poured a hail of fire into the exits, which had become congested by men pausing to orient themselves in No Man's Land. Soon they were totally blocked by dead and wounded. Lieutenant Colonel F.A.C. Hamilton was himself severely wounded while urging those trying to push through to climb the parapet. The second and third waves and part of the fourth did just that only to be 'practically blown back as they went over by machine guns and shrapnel'.

Somehow, enough men were left to assault at 6 pm. Still more remarkable, a few of them reached the wire, and a small party was thought to have penetrated the breastwork near the Wick Salient. Nevertheless, 2/6 Glosters' attack had failed with the loss of 178 men. Were it not for the pipe pusher saps, which were used to evacuate the wounded, the casualties would have been greater.[6]

184 Brigade

As 184 Brigade's two assault battalions, 2/4 Berks and 2/1 Bucks, entered the line on 18 July, they had a grandstand view of the seven-hour British bombardment next day. Major Christie-Miller put a whimsical perspective on the infantry feints that punctuated it:

> *The process was repeated hourly during the 7 hours...which no doubt gave a Biblical flavour to the proceedings, while the shouting and the waving of bayonets took one back to the destruction of the Walls of Jericho.*

But God was not on the side of the gunners supporting 184 Brigade. Inexperienced, their observation obscured by dust and smoke, and

The Sugarloaf bombarded. It remained intact, despite appearances to the contrary. (M. Delebarre)

taking heavy casualties, they made so little impression on the Sugarloaf that a special concentration was ordered at 2.35 pm. It made no difference: 'no effective destructive or neutralising of the Hun infantry, artillery or MGs took place. The total effect of our artillery preparation on the Hun resistance was Nil'.[7]

The German artillery, though, handed out to 184 Brigade the same treatment it had given to the 183rd. Packed behind the breastwork hours before their own bombardment began, 184 Brigade's assault battalions had to weather the German reply from start to finish. 2/4 Berks on the right lost forty men and 2/1 Bucks on the left almost a hundred, which came on top of their casualties in the accidental gassing the night before. Each battalion reinforced its assault companies with a platoon from its reserve company in the 300 Yard Line, forcing a hurried reorganisation an hour before the attack.

Jumping off on the 300-yard frontage from Sutherland Avenue to N.8.c.51/2.31/2, 2/4 Berks were to assault the line held by 12 Company 3/16 BRIR between N.14.a.71/2.3 and N.14.b.11/2.81/2. At 5.40 pm, they debouched from their two sally ports in full view of the German lookouts. 2nd Lieutenant Holzfelder roused his company from its shelters and the machine guns began clattering away. A Company on the left was annihilated and the survivors tried to regain their own breastwork. Emulating Brigadier General Lowry Cole the year before, Lieutenant Colonel John Beer leapt up onto the parapet to rally them and was quickly cut down. Mostly leaderless, the two platoons from B Company that got clear on the right started out for the German wire at 6 pm but found it uncut. Unsupported and under heavy machine gun fire, they too fell back. The attack cost 2/4 Berks 163 casualties.[8]

Attacking between N.8.c.51/2.31/2 and Bond Street on the extreme left of the 61st Division, 2/1 Bucks were to take the Sugarloaf, which was held by 11 Company 3/16 BRIR under 2nd Lieutenant Plenge. With only 120 men between them, A and D Companies had to cover a frontage of almost 400 yards and cross the same 420 yards of open No Man's Land that so worried Elliott. Seeing that the sally ports were death traps, Lieutenant Colonel H.M. Williams switched both companies to Rhondda Sap, giving them a sheltered approach and cutting the length of their assault by almost 200 yards.

11 Company's lookouts had been watching the sap very closely since 3 pm, when they saw some Australian tunnellers trying to fire a pipe-pusher extended from it.

Lieutenant Colonel H.M. Williams.

2/1 BUCKS

3/16 BRIR's view from the Sugarloaf of the ground over which 2/1 Bucks attacked towards it.

Plenge got the artillery onto them, which wounded several before the pipe-pusher was blown at 4.30 pm on the fourth attempt. When the four pitifully thin assault waves crawled over the lip of Rhondda Sap and into No Man's Land at 5.40 pm, shrapnel was falling heavily and the machine gunners were already busy. At 6 pm the attackers leapt up with a cheer and the fire became torrential.

Captain Ivor Stewart-Liberty.

Led by Captain Ivor Stewart-Liberty, D Company on the right, like the 2/4 Berks platoons alongside them, was mown down. Only one man, Lance Corporal Stevens, reached the Sugarloaf. But a few men from A Company on the left, including their commander, Captain Harold Church, were seen on its parapet, which may have prompted the despatch of Captain Henry Buckmaster and C Company at 6.10 pm. The 2/1 Bucks War Diary tersely remarks: 'again, the enemy's machine gun fire prevented any advance without extermination'. 184 Brigade's Vickers guns, three of which were knocked out, expended 30,000 rounds trying to suppress it.

Captain Harold Church.

The war diary also describes how difficult it was to follow the battle as battalion headquarters, located on Picantin Road at N.7.a.6.6, tried to ascertain what had happened to Captain Church's group:

Reports that flowed in...were very contradictory. Owing to the distance between the trenches and to the continuous bombardment and smoke, the officers who were observing found their task almost impossible of fulfilment with any degree of accuracy. Seeing our men actually on the German parapet - it was concluded that a certain number may have got in. But it is certain that very few survived the enemy's machine gun fire, and whether they got in or not – they never returned.

The three companies of 2/1 Bucks that went out suffered

60

244 casualties. Apart from Captain Buckmaster, who collapsed from strain and left for England on 22 July, every officer was either killed or wounded. Church fell close to the Sugarloaf. Sergeant Petty was awarded the Military Medal for dressing Captain Stewart-Liberty's wounds in No Man's Land and carrying him 250 yards to safety under heavy fire.[9]

The 6.30 pm Review

As Mackenzie understood the situation at 6.30 pm, 2/7 Warwicks were on their objective, the attack on the Wick Salient had failed, a small group from 2/4 Glosters were in the German line north of it and 2/1 Bucks had gained a footing in the Sugarloaf. He arranged for the Wick and other parts of the line that had beaten off the assault to be bombarded and told all three brigades to reorganise for a second attempt. Haking approved the use of a reserve battalion from each to support it.

The bombardment of the Wick Salient and the line opposite 183 Brigade started at 7.10 pm and was to last an hour. Those men from 2/6 Warwicks who were pinned down in front of the Wick and could get back to their own line did so. D Company, the battalion's only intact sub-unit, prepared to renew the attack at 8.10 pm, when 183 Brigade would also try again. Further south, A Company, all that remained of 2/7 Warwicks, was ready to break through to Donaldson's group.

Out of touch in 184 Brigade's battle headquarters 1½ miles rearward on the Rue Verte at M.6.a.5.8, Carter instructed Lieutenant Colonel Williams at 6.30 pm to attack again two hours later, sparking an angry exchange between them. The 2/1 Bucks war diary pulls no punches in conveying the frustration Williams, who was in the breastwork, felt on receiving Carter's order 'at a time when every man, save a few telephone operators, orderlies and wounded, was in NO MAN'S LAND'. Christie-Miller recalled: 'It proved next to impossible to persuade the authorities that there was nothing left to attack with'. Eighty men were eventually cobbled together from the remnants of A, C and D Companies, and another forty came from the unused part of B Company in reserve.

In their original orders, 2/1 Bucks were also to have bombed eastwards to link up with 15 Australian Brigade on the far side of the Sugarloaf. On learning that Elliott's attack had failed, Haking directed Mackenzie at 7.30 pm to help the Australians by extending the foothold they both thought 184 Brigade had in the position. In the meantime, Williams had managed to convince Carter that none of his men remained in it. Carter postponed the fresh assault until 9 pm, which would allow an extra half hour's bombardment. In turn, Mackenzie decided to attack with the whole division at 9 pm and extended the bombardment along its entire front in preparation. The Australians had to be told and co-ordination with them arranged. At 7.52 pm Carter sent Mackenzie a message that he wanted passed on to Elliott: 'Am attacking at 9 pm. Can your right battalion co-operate?'[10]

NOTES

1. 61 Div Report; J.J. Shannessy, *History of the 2/6th Royal Warwicks 1914-19* (Cornish Bros, 1929), p. 27.
2. Entry for 19 July 1916, 2/6 Warwicks WD; 'Report on Action of 19th July 1916', 182 Bde WD, Item 23/5, AWM 26.
3. 'Report on Operations 19-7-16', 21 July 1916, 2/7 Warwicks WD, WO95/3056, PRO; Entry for 19 July 1916, 182 MG Coy WD, WO 95/3054, PRO.
4. Report to 183 Bde, 20 July 1916, 2/4 Glosters WD, WO 95/3060, PRO.
5. J.D. Wyatt, 'The Disastrous Attack at Fromelles', *Bristol Evening Post,* 19 July 1960.
6. Entry for 19 July 1916, 2/6 Glosters WD, WO 95/3060, PRO.
7. Christie-Miller, op. cit., p. 181-2.
8. Entry for 19 July 1916, 2/4 Berks WD, WO 95/3065, PRO; F. Loraine Petre, *The Royal Berkshire Regiment. II. 1914-18* (Published by the Regiment, 1925), p. 178.
9. Entry for 19 July 1916, 2/1 Bucks WD, WO 95/3066, PRO; 61 Div Report.
10. Entry for 19 July 1916, 2/1 Bucks WD; Christie-Miller, op. cit., p. 183; *OH*, pp. 391-2.

Grave of Captain Harold Church, Laventie Military Cemetery.

Chapter Five

THE ATTACK OF THE 5TH AUSTRALIAN DIVISION

Like the 61st Division, the Australians sent patrols into No Man's Land on the night of 18/19 July to ascertain the damage the bombardment had done to the German line. The picture that emerged was not encouraging. Several gaps had been cut in the wire in front of 8 Brigade on the left but the defences opposite 14 Brigade in the centre looked intact. On the right, 15 Brigade's patrols could not get close to the German breastwork. The Sugarloaf appeared untouched and its garrison extremely alert. But no great importance was attached to these ominous signs because the main weight of the bombardment had yet to fall.

Accustomed to attacks preceded by a handful of guns laying down a puny fire, the Gallipoli veterans were awed when the shelling intensified after 1 pm. The newcomers were overwhelmed. Sergeant Les Martin of 8 Machine Gun Company told his brother:

From about 11 am till 6 pm there was not a space of a second's duration when some of our guns were not firing, the row

As seen from 53 Battalion's line (foreground), smoke rises from shells bursting on 3/21 BRIR'S line opposite.

*was deafening. I put wadding in my ears while we were down in
the supports waiting to go forward . . . some of the batteries were
about a hundred yards away and they barked incessantly all day
long.*[1]

Before leaving their billets at Bac St. Maur for the Rue Quesnoy,
Private Charles Johnston and the rest of 56 Battalion whiled away the
time by watching the display. 'The forward area was shrouded in a pall
of dust and smoke and shell bursts, and we believed no man could live
in such an inferno', Sergeant H.R. Williams of A Company wrote.
Obviously reassured, he and his mates relaxed with a pre-battle drink.

> *We entered an estaminet, and found the place crowded to
> overflowing. Madame and her assistants were hard pressed to
> cope with the rush. The men were in the best of spirits and looked
> forward to the attack as if it were a football match. All talk was
> of the 'stunt' and the women of the estaminet knew the details as
> well as we did.*[2]

Friendly Fire

For the assault companies that had stayed in the line, the main danger
came from the erratic shooting of the Australian artillery. 'Dropshorts'
pelted them, particularly in 8 Brigade and on the left of 14 Brigade,
where the narrowness of No Man's Land left no room for error. One
stray round pulped an engineer party working on the front line parapet.
The assault companies withdrawn when the attack was postponed on
17 July left their billets shortly after noon. Each man carried 150
rounds of ammunition, two grenades and two sandbags and every third
man a pick or shovel.

The German artillery observers in Fromelles church and on the

The view from Fromelles church then . . .

ridge did not need binoculars to see the long columns snaking forward. At 2.15 pm, their guns began drenching the 300 Yard and support lines and the communication trenches. When the final stage of the British bombardment began at 3 pm, they hit the front line as well. 31 Battalion's ammunition dump blew up and shrapnel peppered the commanding officer, Lieutenant Colonel Frederick Toll. A Boer War veteran whose son had fallen at Gallipoli, Toll stayed on. *Minenwerfers* caved in Mine Avenue near the front line at N.10.c.3.6. In the centre, 53 Battalion lost fifty men and both Pinney's Avenue and Brompton Road were blown in. 15 Brigade on the right and VC and Cellar Farm Avenues on the outer flanks were also knocked about.

15 Brigade reported its four waves in place at 3.25 pm, 14 and 8 Brigades at 3.45 pm and 4 pm respectively. Despite arriving later than McCay's 3 pm deadline, they still had two hours to wait, packed shoulder-to-shoulder in the trenches and huddled behind the breastwork. The German gunners took every advantage of the overcrowding and their fire did not ease until 5 pm. It intensified again when they thought that the feint lift in the bombardment at 5.21 pm signalled the start of the attack. The support line and communication trenches were hardest hit.

Dropshorts were landing on 8 and 14 Brigades all the while. Observing the fall of shot of each gun, the only foolproof way of correcting the problem, was impossible during a bombardment and it worsened as the tempo stepped up. The casualties from the shelling of both sides in 31 Battalion forced Toll to combine its third and fourth waves into a single wave. 32 Battalion was also badly hit and 54 Battalion, yet to complete its first day in the line, lost three of its four company commanders and their deputies.

... and now as the morning mist starts to lift.

UE DU BOIS   AUSTRALIAN MEMORIAL PARK   RUE PETILLON

Fighting Spirit

As the Germans seemed to be getting a far worse battering, morale held. The Australians cheered on seeing ragged gaps being torn in the enemy's breastwork. 'Wire netting and woodwork was observed flying through the air' after a large explosion opposite 15 Brigade and even the erstwhile gloomy Elliott, sharing the danger in the front line, was sufficiently impressed to assure his men, 'Boys, you won't find a German in the trenches when you get there.'[3] But at 5.10 pm, too late for the artillery to respond, a message arrived at 15 Brigade headquarters warning that the entanglements west of the Laies, which protected the side of the Sugarloaf facing Elliott's men, were uncut. Observers in 60 Battalion saw three intact machine gun emplacements there.

The German garrisons were also seen to ignore the feint lifts. Their lookouts realised immediately that the blowing of whistles and waving of bayonets and dummy figures were just ruses, and of such a transparent nature, according to 30 Battalion's history, as to cause more amusement than anxiety. During the final feint, the area behind 14 Brigade came alive. As Brompton Road was so packed that moving along it was impossible, the third wave climbed out at 5.25 pm and hurried across the fields towards the front line, followed by the fourth wave six minutes later. At the same time, the 61st Division began exiting its sally ports and the British bombardment increased. The German counter-bombardment switched to the front and 300 Yard Lines, creating a surreal scene:

> The first thing that struck you was that shells were bursting everywhere, mostly high-explosive; and you could see machine-guns knocking bits off the trees in front of the reserve line and sparking against the wire . . . When men looked over the top they saw No Man's Land leaping up everywhere in showers of dust and sand.[4]

16 and 21 BRIR cheered as the Australians clambered over the parapet. Their fighting spirit had proved as resilient as the Australian, their machine guns had not been knocked out and almost four hours of daylight remained.

15 Brigade

15 Brigade's leading wave deployed at 5.45 pm. Sporadic rifle fire was heard at 5.50 pm when the second wave left and a machine gun opened from the Sugarloaf as the third followed five minutes later. At 6.02 pm, after the barrage had lifted, the firing increased. Through the smoke

The Laies as crossed by 15 Brigade.

and dust hanging over No Man's Land, men were seen near the German breastwork at 6.09 pm. At 6.15 pm, the firing subsided. From his battle headquarters at Trou Post, Elliott reported at 6.30 pm that the attack appeared successful. In reality, Plenge's company and 10 Company 3/16 BRIR under 2nd Lieutenant Bachschneider had destroyed it between them.

A few German riflemen had started firing as the Australians cleared their parapet and a machine gun joined in when they moved through the wire. But then some grassy broken ground sheltered 59 Battalion on the right and screened 60 Battalion crossing the Laies alongside. Only two feet deep, the brook was no obstacle but it ran towards the Sugarloaf, from which much of the fire came, and the leading wave inevitably gravitated in that direction. The attackers were now in the open and in enfilade to the Sugarloaf on their right flank.

10 and 11 Companies began a fusillade so devastating that they were thought to be manning their parapet with one man per yard. They 'swept a hail of bullets in our faces, like a veritable blizzard', Lieutenant Knyvett, 15 Brigade's Intelligence Officer, recalled. 'The first wave went down like wheat before the reaper'. Hit as soon as it topped the parapet, the second got about half way across No Man's Land. Seeing no movement ahead, the third wave pressed on towards where it imagined the first two must have been lying ready for the final rush. It was also shattered. Wounded and pinned down 150 yards from the German parapet, Lieutenant Tom Kerr of 60 Battalion saw the occupants standing shoulder high above it, 'looking as if they were wondering what was coming next'. The fourth wave gave them their answer and they obliterated it. A

Lieutenant Tom Kerr. (M. Wood)

67

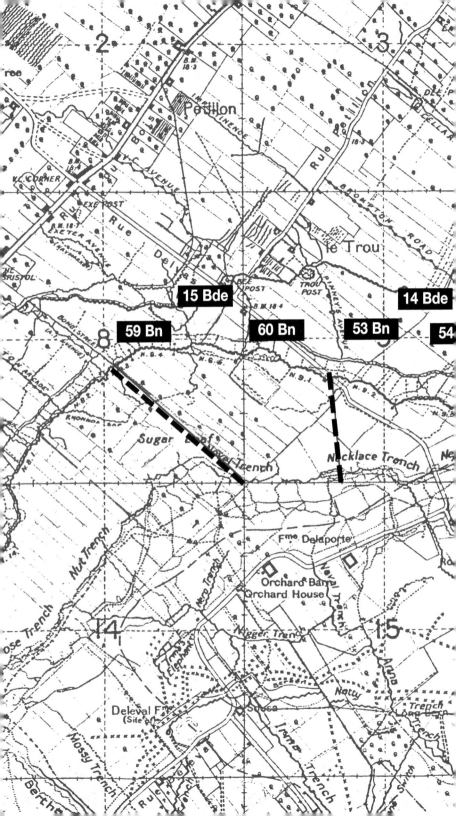

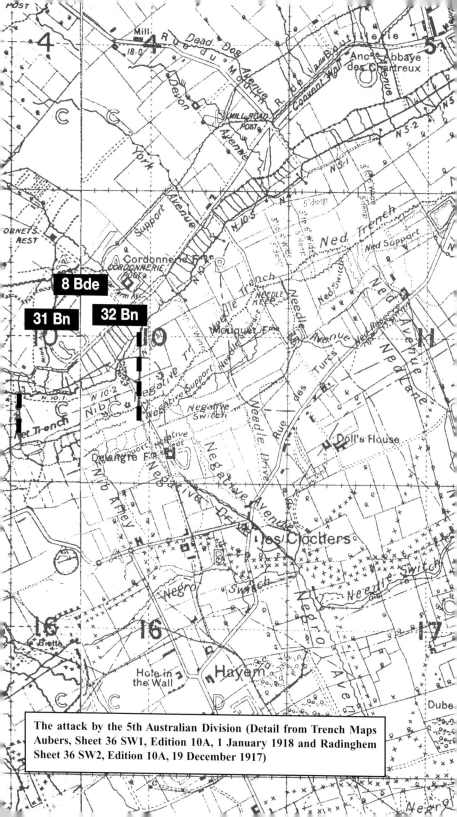

The attack by the 5th Australian Division (Detail from Trench Maps Aubers, Sheet 36 SW1, Edition 10A, 1 January 1918 and Radinghem Sheet 36 SW2, Edition 10A, 19 December 1917)

3/16 BRIR's view from the Sugarloaf of the ground over which 15 Brigade attacked.

machine gun firing down the Laies turned the brook into a deathtrap.

Sergeant Walter Downing's impressions of 60 Battalion's attack vividly convey how deadly the grazing fire from the Sugarloaf was:

> *The 60th climbed on the parapet, heavily laden, dragging with them scaling ladders, light bridges, picks, shovels, and bags of bombs.*
>
> *Scores of stammering German machine-guns spluttered violently, drowning the noise of the cannonade. The air was thick with bullets, swishing in a flat lattice of death. There were gaps in the lines of men – wide ones, small ones. The survivors spread across the front, keeping the line straight...The bullets skimmed low, from knee to groin, riddling the tumbling bodies before they touched the ground. Still the line kept on.*
>
> *Hundreds were mown down in the flicker of an eyelid, like great rows of teeth knocked from a comb, but still the line went on, thinning and stretching. Wounded wriggled into shellholes or were hit again. Men were cut in two by streams of bullets. And still the line went on.*

A and C Companies had made up the first two waves, B and D Companies the third and fourth. The right flank, which was closer to the Sugarloaf, dwindled rapidly and no-one got further than Kerr's small group and survived. A few men on the extreme left may have entered the German breastwork. If so, 10 Company quickly overwhelmed them. Of the four company commanders, three were dead and the fourth badly wounded. Most of the other officers were also hit. McCrae and battalion headquarters had gone out with D Company. He was shot through the neck eighty yards from his own parapet. Twenty-one year old Major Tom Elliott, whom Elliott (no relation) had wanted in brigade headquarters but left as 60 Battalion's second-in-command at McCrae's urging, was mortally wounded in the chest while encouraging D Company onward.[5]

The story was the same in 59 Battalion. Knowing what awaited

GERMAN FRONT LINE

them, the handful of able-bodied remaining rose and charged the German wire the instant the barrage lifted. Some fell instantly; others on the wire itself. Commanding A Company, which was closest to the Sugarloaf, and hit in the head at the start of the attack, Captain Aubrey Liddelow led a small group onto the German parapet and was hit again in the shoulder and arm. Seeing that they were alone, he withdrew them into a shell hole, where one of his men, who was also wounded, implored Liddelow to return with him for medical attention. He sent the man back but stayed himself, saying, 'I'll never walk back into safety and leave the men I have led into such grave danger – we'll wait for reinforcements'. A German shell killed him a few minutes later.[6]

Captain Aubrey Liddelow.

When Elliott sent his success message at 6.30 pm, thirty five of the thirty nine assaulting officers and most of the NCO's were casualties. The leading elements of 59 Battalion were entrenching in a shallow depression 100 yards from the German breastwork. In old agricultural furrows ninety yards from it, 60 Battalion was also burrowing frantically. Behind them, those who had not been able to get so far forward sheltered in shell holes or in the undulations of the once cultivated flats. Many wounded lay in the open. The Germans gave particular attention to the engineers extending VC and Pinney's Avenues across No Man's Land. 15 Machine Gun Company, which tried to suppress the Sugarloaf from its location between 184 and 15 Brigades, had lost heavily in the counter-bombardment before the attack.[7]

Elliott's first intimation that his assault had been shot to earth did not arrive until 6.40 pm. Sent back by his commanding officer, Lieutenant Colonel E.A. Harris, 59 Battalion's second-in-command, Major Herbert Layh, brought the gloomy news that it was stalled half way

Major Herbert Layh.

across No Man's Land. Then some returning wounded from 60 Battalion stated that they had reached the second line fifty yards beyond the German breastwork and that 14 Brigade had been successful on the left. Thinking that only the 59th had failed, Elliott sent Layh back with a message for Harris to try again. He also told Lieutenant David Doyle, 60 Battalion's Intelligence Officer, to find McCrae. But McCrae was already dead.

Confronted by the 'most awful scene of slaughter imaginable', Doyle could only locate Layh, who reiterated that the attack had collapsed. Doyle informed Elliott at 7.06 pm and, as more information trickled in, Elliott gave McCay a truer picture of the situation at 7.18 pm: 'The trenches are full of the enemy. Every man who rises is shot down. Reports from wounded indicate that the attack is failing for want of support'. On hearing that Harris was shell-shocked by a near miss, he put Layh in charge of 59 Battalion. Blown into a water-filled shell hole shortly afterwards, Layh was himself shell-shocked but remained in command.[8]

14 Brigade

Attacking between Pinney's Avenue and N.10.c.$^1/_2$.6, 14 Brigade was to capture the German line from N.9.c.7.1 to N.10.c.$^1/_2$.2$^1/_2$, a stretch held

A soldier from A Company, 53 Battalion poses for Lance Corporal Charles Lorking just before going over.

by 11 and 12 Companies of 3/21 BRIR. The Rue Delvas turned due south to bisect it, forming a convenient boundary for 53 and 54 Battalions on the right and left respectively. 53 Battalion had the harder task, even though Colonel Pope was advised at 5.20 pm that Delaporte Farm, 250 yards beyond the German front line in its sector, had been dropped as an objective. Whereas 54 Battalion only had to go 100 yards, No Man's Land in front of the 53rd was 250 yards across and swept by 'Parapet Joe', a notoriously accurate German machine gunner. Lance Corporal Charles Lorking was very conscious of him when he snapped the German line under bombardment and eight men of A Company having a last cigarette. All but three would be killed, and those three wounded.

72

Only three of the eight men from A Company 53 Battalion in this photograph survived the battle. All three were wounded.

The two leading waves had lost the equivalent of two platoons to the counter-bombardment when the first wave left at 5.43 pm. A Company on the right was immediately struck in enfilade by that part of 3/16 BRIR's line that should have been overcome by 60 Battalion. A machine gun, possibly 'Parapet Joe', firing down the Rue Delvas from

'Parapet Joe's' view down the Rue Delvas. VC Corner Cemetery in the background.

VC CORNER AUSTRALIAN
CEMETERY MEMORIAL

53 BATTALION

the western end of today's Australian Memorial Park, also proved deadly until 54 Battalion silenced it. A Company pressed through the fire to the German breastwork, where 12 Company held it up until the second wave arrived.

B Company on the left and A and B Companies of 54 Battalion's first wave alongside got across 'in perfect order'. Although the bombardment had cut the wire, the breastwork, marked out today by the fence on the northern side of the Australian Memorial Park, was little damaged. But the Australians arrived as 11 Company was emerging to man it. In hand-to-hand fighting, they killed most of them and captured two machine guns while clearing the concrete shelters in the breastwork and the *Wohngraben* ten yards in rear.

Ten yards further and roughly on the line of the blockhouses in the Memorial Park, the Australians found *Wohngraben* whose facilities amazed them and behind which ran a light tramway. Lieutenant Colonel Cass established 54 Battalion's headquarters in one located about fifty yards past the fence at the eastern end:

> [It] *was fitted with electric light, had two sleeping berths end to end giving a length in the side of about 13 or 14 feet, height about 7'6", width 8 feet. Thickness of earth on top about 8 feet, depth (below ground level) of about 10 feet. It was reached by steps and had a passage or light to a window. It was strongly built and had an upright about 12" x 12" in the centre supporting a rafter of somewhat similar thickness. The ceiling appeared to be flat sheet iron papered with wallpaper. The walls were papered and even decorated with gold moulding similar to picture frame moulding. It had table, armchair, heating stove, electric bell, acetylene gas lamp similar to bicycle lamp. In it were stored 10 to 20 thousand rounds S.A.A., many flares, gas helmets...Other dugouts in the line were similarly built.*[9]

The first news came, as it did in 15 Brigade, from returning wounded, who reported at 6.27 pm that the leading wave had taken the first line with slight loss. Twenty minutes later a signalling disc indicating the fall of the second line was seen. C and D Companies from 55 Battalion began carrying sandbags and ammunition to the captured position, the extension of Brompton's Road to it was started, and 14 Machine Gun Company sent ten machine guns across. Pope thought things were going well. In fact, the attack had already run into trouble.

Casualties were indeed low but they included most of the principals. Lieutenant Colonel Ignatius Norris, 53 Battalion's commanding officer, yelled, 'Come on lads! Only another trench to take', as he was killed on the German parapet. Major Victor Sampson, who led C Company, fell shortly afterwards. As Norris' deputy was acting as a liaison officer to Pope, command of the 53rd devolved to 21 year-old Captain Charles Arblaster of D Company. In 54 Battalion, Cass was the only senior officer left. Major Roy Harrison, his deputy, had died in the first wave. All the company commanders, their deputies and six platoon commanders were casualties, half of them before leaving the Australian line. The advance to the support line was therefore largely leaderless.

Once over the breastwork, the following waves expected to see ahead of them the trenches of the second line and the support line. Instead, overgrown fields, pockmarked by shell holes and cut by hedges and trees, stretched towards Aubers Ridge. Thinking that the trenches must be hidden in the grassland, the Australians struck out across it, 'like sportsmen after quail, occasionally shooting at Germans who had settled in shellholes and who now started up to run farther'.[10] They passed over some fragmentary trenches and two ditches containing a couple of feet of water, before going through their own artillery fire to reach the Rue Delvas as it swung sharp left at Rouge Bancs 300 yards behind the front line. Some men went another 600 yards, nearing the blockhouse at N.16.c.1.1, where Adolf Hitler may have sheltered while running messages.

The advance had become hopelessly scattered well before the few surviving officers realised that the second and third German trenches either did not exist or else were denoted by the two ditches they had crossed. They pulled the nearest men back to the second ditch and 54 Battalion set up most of the posts along it. As German shelling and burning farms and villages thickened the smoke and dust thrown up by the Australian barrage, the process was anything but orderly.

53 Battalion's posts were strung out on a line that began at the Rue Delvas 75 yards short of its junction with the track past Delaporte Farm, and ran parallel to the track for 200 yards. Because of the heavy fire coming from 60 Battalion's area, it bent back at that point towards the old German front line. The losses this fire inflicted on A and C Companies, combined with the casualties before the assault, left the posts thinly manned and communications between them tenuous. Arblaster thought he was in touch with 60 Battalion and had intermittent contact across the Rue Delvas with 54 Battalion, which had withdrawn to the first ditch at 7 pm owing to persistent shelling of the second ditch by the Australian artillery. Its line parallelled the road's eastward swing to link with 8 Brigade at N.10.c.0.1, near the

14 Brigade's right flank, held by Captain Arblaster and 53 Battalion.

German front line just west of the farm track and close to where a clump of bushes hides two blockhouses today.

Around 6.30 pm, bombing erupted on 53 Battalion's right as the Germans, probably a mixed force from 10 Company 3/16 BRIR and 12 Company 3/21 BRIR under 2nd Lieutenant Bachschneider, struck. Aware now that they and not 60 Battalion were his neighbours, Arblaster left Captain J.J. Murray, who led B Company, in charge on the Rue Delvas while he organised the defence of the exposed flank. Unknown to Arblaster, the Germans were also attacking along their old front line, which was empty apart from a few A Company bombers left behind by 53 Battalion's leading wave when it took off for the support line. Outnumbered and with only seven men unwounded, the bombers' commander ordered his men to throw their remaining grenades and withdraw.

As often happens in such circumstances, word spread rapidly, and the wounded in No Man's Land, the men digging the communication trench and some in the old Australian line took up the cry to retire. The imposing 6'4" frame of Gallipoli veteran Captain Norman Gibbins steadied them as he led A and B Companies of 55 Battalion forward from the 300 Yard Line to garrison it. Neither Arblaster nor Cass knew what had happened or realised the precarious situation behind them. But Cass did know that he needed more men. 14 Brigade's war diary records that at 7.36 pm:

> *54th Battalion asked for reinforcements stating that the Bn of the 8th Brigade on its left had apparently withdrawn, but that he was consolidating his left. Permission was obtained from 5 Division to use 2 coys 55th Bn to support 53rd and 54th Bns. This 1/2 Bn of 55th was now in our old front line, its remainder having been used up for working parties. Col McConaghy [CO 55 Bn] was ordered to send one company in support of the 53rd Bn and one in support of the 54th.*[11]

76

ADVANCED LINE 53 BATTALION

Both companies were in position by 9.30 pm, A Company under Gibbins on the left of 54 Battalion and B Company, commanded by Lieutenant J.H. Matthews, on the left of the 53rd.

8 Brigade

Brigadier General Tivey had chosen the 31st and 32nd Battalions for 8 Brigade's assault because they were the toughest units in a formation with few veterans in its ranks. Queensland miners and bush workers were common in 31 Battalion, while 32 Battalion, commanded by Lieutenant Colonel D.M. Coghill, boasted many Western and South Australian miners. Though the two battalions had been battered by the artillery of both sides while waiting to attack, the German front line, held by 10 Company 3/21 BRIR, was closer opposite them than anywhere else.

A and C Companies in 31 Battalion's first wave went over between N.10.c.1/2.6 and N.10.c.51/2.61/2 at 5.58 pm followed by its second wave on the barrage lift two minutes later. Losses were high as 10 Company fought hard initially but when the first wave closed with its objective, the 250 yards of breastwork from N.10.c.1/2.21/2 to N.10.c.51/2.31/2, it met only a few men covering a hasty retreat. Going around a traverse, Lieutenant Drayton bumped into an officer clutching a grenade and shot him. Private Percy Weakley saw a machine gun crew about to leave its gun and killed four before shrapnel bursting overhead killed him.

The leading waves had moved on when Lieutenant Colonel Toll arrived in the German front line with the combined third and fourth waves. Leaving some men to help the Lewis gunners get established, he set out after them and struck the same problem that had confounded Cass:

> [We] *swept on with the intention of capturing the second and third trenches in the first line system, but we went on and on but no trace could be found of same. It now appeared evident that the*

77

information supplied as to enemy defences and aerial photographs was incorrect and misleading. The ground was flat, covered with fairly long grass, the trenches shown on aerial photos were nothing but ditches full of water...

As they continued, Lieutenant Trounson saved a German trapped in one of these ditches from the attentions of an Australian who prodded him back under with his bayonet every time he surfaced for air. Toll called a halt when the advance was engaged by a machine gun cleverly concealed at the Hofgarten strongpoint near Les Clochers, 650 yards to the southeast. At 6.30 pm he sent a carrier pigeon to Tivey with the message: 'Four waves well over 200 yards beyond enemy's parapet. No enemy works found yet so am digging in'. At this stage, his right was at N.10.c.7.1, well to the east of 14 Brigade's left and out of touch with it. There was no sign of 32 Battalion either.

Leaving his deputy in charge, Toll and some of his staff braved the Australian barrage to confirm that the German support line did not lie ahead. Reaching the Rue Delvas opposite the pond at N.16.a.4.5, he saw the Grashof strongpoint further on and advanced groups of 14 Brigade off to the west. Unable to contact them, Toll returned to his own line. It was now under fire from machine guns at Delangré Farm, towards which German reserves were seen moving, being shelled by the Germans and hit by Australian 'dropshorts'. Its flanks were still in the air.

As the only defensible position seemed to be the old German front line, Toll withdrew 31 Battalion to it. Lieutenant Drayton in the right hand post linked with 54 Battalion near the farm track and set up another post fifty yards ahead for early warning. Toll also left B Company under Captain Charles Mills as a screen in the ditch where most of the battalion had taken cover from the Hofgarten machine gun. The ditch ran intermittently northeastwards in the field east of the farm track and through the northern part of the thick copse that blocks the view of Delangré Farm from this location today. B Company's line started close to the western side of the copse. Unknown to Mills, a 300-yard gap separated it from 54 Battalion's left flank. Unknown to Toll and Mills, 32 Battalion held the same ditch further east. Toll reported: 'Can hold enemy's first line if reinforcements are sent over urgently'.[12]

Starting between N.10.c.51/2.61/2 and Cellar Farm Avenue, 32 Battalion, which had spent less than a day in the trenches, anchored the left flank of the whole attack. It was to seize 3/21 BRIR's front line as far east as the Kastenweg, the communication trench in which the Kensingtons held out in 1915. The assault troops also thought they had to take Delangré Farm because a last minute order deleting this

3/21 BRIR's view of the ground over which 32 Battalion attacked.

objective did not reach them in time. A switch trench dug by A Company 30 Battalion and the engineers would become part of the new Australian front line. It was to start in 60 Brigade's sector, from which suppressive fire would be laid down and gas released against 9 Company 3/21 BRIR further left to prevent it enfilading the attack. The extension of the bombardment over its line and the mine explosion at N.10.d.1.8 were also supposed to help.

None of these precautions worked. The wind was unfavourable for gas and neither the bombardment nor the fire from 60 Brigade could stifle 9 Company. Mouquet Farm and the Tadpole were active immediately and losses among the leaders in the first wave, which went over at 5.53 pm, were heavy. They included Major John Higgon, the attached British regular commanding A Company on the left. The mine blast at 6 pm made no difference as 10 Company continued to man its parapet. Its daring in trying to halt the Australians was later commented upon.

Heading into the fields beyond, the following waves inclined towards the ruins of Delangré Farm, to which 10 Company had withdrawn. The fire from it was severe and, without their Lewis Guns, the Australians could not properly reply. Captain A.R. White, D

The ruins of Delangré Farm. (M. Delebarre)

KASTENWEG

BRITISH MINES

AUSTRALIAN FRONT LINE

DELANGRÉ FARM

MINENWERFER PIT

AUSTRALIAN MINE

LES CLOCHERS

GERMAN
FRONT LINE

Aerial view of the left flank taken after the attack. (M. Delebarre)

80

Company's commander and one of the few officers left, looked for the second and third trenches, which were prominently marked amidst a maze of connecting alleys on his map. Apart from a water-filled switch trench, he could see only the usual muddy ditches in the grass. White ordered his men to establish a line in some shell holes and the farther of two ditches beside the Kastenweg. From there they eventually met the advanced line of 31 Battalion near N.10.c.7.3. Like Toll, Lieutenant Colonel Coghill sought reinforcements but Tivey, who had no authority to send them, could only tell him to hold on 'at all costs'.[13]

Hit in the arm and leg, Lieutenant Samuel Mills and some bombers blocked the Kastenweg at N.10.c.9.4, seventy-five yards north of Delangré Farm, and a machine gun was sited there with a post in front to warn of any German move along it. Barricades were set up east of the Kastenweg's junction with the front line and parties from A Company 30 Battalion started the switch trench. But the upturned edges of the mine crater gave as little protection to the diggers as they did to the assault. Sergeant Charles Garland, who was to erect a sign on the parapet showing the easternmost point captured, Second Lieutenant John Lees, marking the course to be dug across No Man's Land, and most of those with them were soon killed.

A machine gunner near the Tadpole, who had seen Lees' party leave, slaughtered the next groups that followed it through the wire, including the engineer officer in charge of the digging, Second Lieutenant Christian Tenbosch. Noticing that the fixed elevation of the gun prevented it firing below knee height, Captain R.A. Allen, A Company's second-in-command, used the dead as cover while pushing forward sandbags to make a screen, finally allowing the work to get underway.

Consolidation

At 7.30 pm, the line 8 and 14 Brigades held was disjointed, and its right flank hung in the air. The muddy ditches they occupied, some of them part of the system draining the fields, were where the German second and third lines once ran. Both had been abandoned when the rising Laies flooded them in autumn 1915, and the thinning out of the front line garrison after the improvements to the breastwork made their reclamation unnecessary. Thereafter they served as sumps for the water pumped out of the *Wohngraben*. Pumping machinery was noted at more than one point in the captured area.

While the maps showed the system as it had been, the aerial photographs taken before the battle gave a clue as to how it actually was. Lined with earth-filled ammunition chests, the Kastenweg, 'Chest

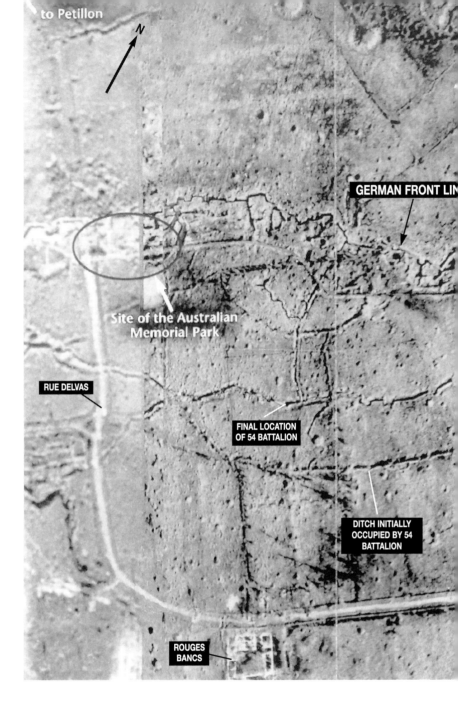

to Petillon

N

GERMAN FRONT LIN

Site of the Australian
Memorial Park

RUE DELVAS

FINAL LOCATION
OF 54 BATTALION

DITCH INITIALLY
OCCUPIED BY 54
BATTALION

ROUGES
BANCS

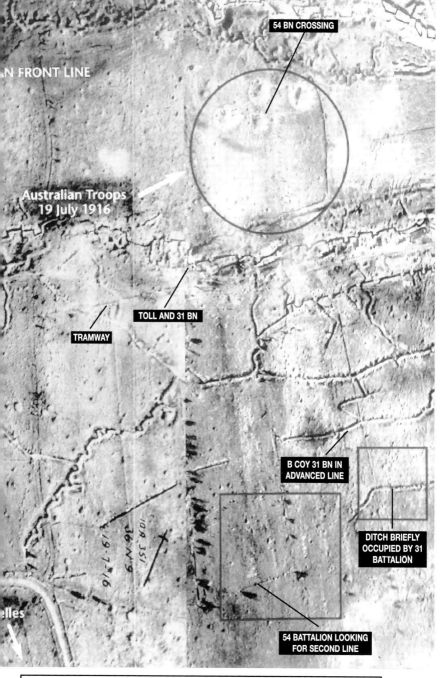

54 BN CROSSING

N FRONT LINE

Australian Troops
19 July 1916

TOLL AND 31 BN

TRAMWAY

B COY 31 BN IN
ADVANCED LINE

DITCH BRIEFLY
OCCUPIED BY 31
BATTALION

54 BATTALION LOOKING
FOR SECOND LINE

lles

A composite of aerial photographs of the ground over which 8 and 14 Brigades attacked. Those taken during the battle show the early positions taken up by both brigades before they pulled back to ditches closer to the German breastwork. This sequence is also displayed at the entrance to the Australian Memorial Park.

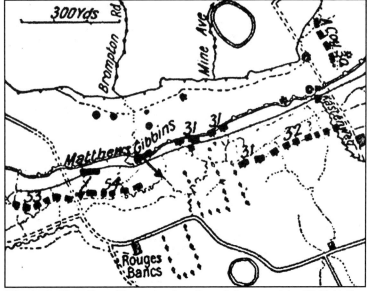

The Australian dispositions, showing the reinforcement by 55 Battalion and the switch trench dug by 30 Battalion (Detail from *The Australian Imperial Force in France 1916*, p. 403).

Way', stood out as having been built over the old trenches, which would not have happened were they still in use. The Australians lacked photographic interpreters but they might have drawn the right conclusion had there been time for close study of the pictures before the attack. But Haking's headquarters did not pick up the mistake either. As Lieutenant Knyvett remarked afterward, 'a great number of men were lost by going too far into enemy territory, seeking the supposed third line'.[14]

Nor did the consequences stop there. Had the trenches been serviceable, the Australians could have made a new parapet facing the Germans simply by transferring the sandbags from the old parapet at the front to the back. Instead, they stood in knee-deep water, trying to fill the few sandbags they had with soil so clayey, recalled Private Tom Donnellan of 30 Battalion, that it 'clung to the shovel like an oyster, necessitating removal by hand, and when filled into sandbags and placed on the parapet it became slippery as an eel and could not be kept in position'. As shell-bursts choked the Laies, the water rose higher and mud scooped from the ditches had to be used. Toll called the job 'heartbreaking'.[15]

As the work went on, the German artillery shelled the pocket continuously. The Australian gunners, uncertain of the exact line occupied, shelled it too, and sometimes as far back as the old German front line. Maintaining a telephone link throughout, 32 Battalion asked for so many lifts that by 7.50 pm the gunners had lengthened their range by 500 yards and McCay asked Tivey to make sure the troublesome shelling was not German. Then the German guns scored direct hits on two more ammunition dumps and Toll gave the gas alarm as dense smoke rolled across the battlefield. The haze that already shrouded it became an acrid fog, making communication between the groups in the ditches even more difficult. Night was also falling.

By this time the third battalions were garrisoning the Australian front line and the fourth battalions had moved into the 300 Yard Line, all wearing felt hats instead of helmets. Terrible sights greeted them. Lieutenant Zander's enthusiasm was an early casualty when 30 Battalion took over 8 Brigade's sector:

> *Dead seemed to be everywhere – one man had got a hit from a shell and half his face was blown away. He lay across the duckboard track, blocking it. A sergeant stepped forward and shifted him to one side, while another person covered the dead man's face with a bloodstained tunic. It seemed all so terrible to us - these dead lying all around - but we were not used to the sight of dead then.*

Sergeant Williams' experience as 56 Battalion headed into the maelstrom on the opposite flank was no less depressing:

> *The German shelling and machine-gun fire had now reached terrific volume. Brompton Avenue had in places ceased to exist as a defined work; the bodies of dead men lay thickly along its length. Here the supporting battalion [55 Battalion] moving up, had suffered severely in the passage. The German shells still searched this sap and blew great craters along its length as we struggled through, trampling underfoot the dead that cluttered it. All the while we were losing men. Some of the wounded lay in pools staining the water with their blood. Dead men, broken trench-material, shattered duckboards that tripped us as we passed, the smell of the fumes of high explosives, and the unforgettable odour of death made this trench a place of horror.*

Sapper Sidney Donnan and his mates decided that 14 Brigade's old line was too dangerous:

> *The slaughter and confusion being worse than ever we decided to go over into the German lines and do something. Getting over the parapet we found No Man's Land a sort of hell on earth mainly through the moans of the wounded who were too numerous to get away, and the barrage was too heavy.*

An NCO helping to take 53 Battalion's Lewis guns over recalled:

The moment they cleared the top of the parapet it became hideous with machine-gun fire. There was a slight slope – our line ran down it, and then went splash into the ditch up to their waists in water. It was slimy, but it gave some protection...About forty yards along it the leader got hit in the neck by a machine gun bullet. He choked – one of the gunners tied him up, and, with another, they lay there for half-an-hour or longer. The ditch was full of wounded and dying men – like a butcher's shop – men groaning and crying and shrieking. Ammunition was being carried up by pairs of men, the boxes being carried on sticks. One man would go down and crash would go the box into the water. Shelling was very heavy.

Two of the four machine gun crews crossing with Sergeant Martin to support 8 Brigade did not make it. Around him too, 'You could hear the moans of the wounded and dying wherever you went'. Sheltering in a German dugout, which was proof against all but a 'well aimed or rather lucky shell', he lamented the lack of decent dugouts in his own line, where 'a shell hitting anywhere near the parapet...has a good chance of catching a few'.[16]

As ammunition, grenades, sandbags, picks and shovels were all desperately needed, the carrying parties from 30 and 55 Battalions faced the daunting prospect of having to go back and forth between the two lines. Most did not. On reaching the old German line, they were sent to the scattered groups entrenching in the ditches, whose commanders welcomed them as much as their loads. Instead of going back for another load, they were set to work digging and soon became involved in the fighting.

30 Battalion lost nearly all of its carriers in this way, Zander remarking in his inimitable style, 'They wanted to stop there and box on with their chums in the 31st and 32nd'. Sergeant Stevenson of B Company put it more prosaically: 'The thought of being hit in the back on the return journey was too much for us, hence our inclination to remain with the fighting troops'.[17] At the other extreme, the more experienced men knew how important their job was and kept at it all night. Sergeant A. Panton of 55 Battalion crossed No Man's Land at least a dozen times.

Preparing To Strike Back
Like any force defending a position, the Germans had a counter-penetration plan to contain their attackers and a counterattack plan to regain lost ground. Thanks to Second Lieutenant Bachschneider's

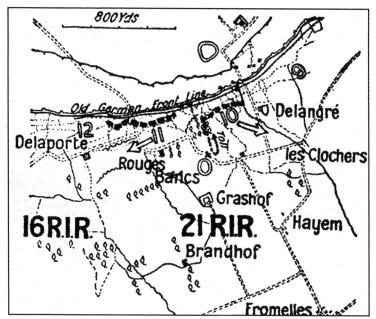

The German company dispositions on the Australian frontage and the point reached by Lieutenant Colonel Toll (Detail from *The Australian Imperial Force in France 1916*, p. 399).

initiative in quickly throwing together a group to take on Captain Arblaster's men, the counter-penetration plan was hardly tested on the Australian right flank. Four platoons from 2/16 BRIR, which was manning the strongpoints on the Rue Deleval, were still sent there. On the left, 10 Company 3/21 BRIR had barricaded the Kastenweg near Delangré Farm and reinforced its garrison. 21 BRIR also held the Türkenecke strongpoint at N.16.b.2.7 and four platoons from 20 BRIR were at Les Clochers.

At the same time, units that had long practised moving up from their support and reserve locations were setting the counterattack plan in motion. Before nightfall, 9 Company, part of 20 BRIR's reserve, arrived from le Maisnil to join 2/21 BRIR, which was 21 BRIR's support battalion, 6 Company from its reserve and 1/21 BRIR from the brigade reserve, in retaking the left flank. 1/20 BRIR from the divisional reserve was also coming from Fournes but a pasting from the artillery delayed it near Fromelles. The assault would be launched simultaneously with one co-ordinated by 16 BRIR on the opposite flank.

As the bombardment intensified, 16 BRIR's commander had moved to his battle headquarters at Bayern Nord on the outskirts of Fromelles at 5.30 pm and received word of the British and Australian break-ins at 7 pm. 182 Brigade's penetration was quickly established as not being

Bayern Nord today.

serious but the Australians had reportedly taken some strongpoints beyond the front line. Three companies from 1/16 BRIR, which was in brigade reserve, were returned to the regiment to counterattack them, along with 16 BRIR's own reserve, a composite company of 2/16 BRIR under Second Lieutenant Arnold that had gone from Fromelles to the Heckengraben, a communication trench leading to Delaporte Farm. Adolf Hitler delivered messages pertaining to the attack.

Support was also available from outside the 6th BR Division. Crown Prince Rupprecht of Bavaria, the commander of the Sixth Army, sent it 3/104 Regiment, a Saxon outfit from XIX Corps near Armentières, 25 Jäger Battalion from XXVII Reserve Corps and two heavy artillery batteries. Before the German counterattack got underway, the Australians assaulted again in the most tragic and controversial episode of the battle.

NOTES

1. Martin to Jack, 31 July 1916, Item 12/11/1587, 1DRL/0483, AWM.
2. H. R. Williams, *The Gallant Company,* (Angus & Robertson, 1933), p.55.
3. 'Summary of Messages Received 19/20 July 1916', Appendix B to 5 Div War D, Item 1/50, Roll 836, AWM 4; *OH*, p. 362.
4. Sloan, op. cit., p. 72; *OH*, p. 358.
5. R.H. Knyvett, *Over There with the Australians* (Hodder and Stoughton, 1918), pp. 153-4; OH, pp. 365-6; W.H. Downing, *To The Last Ridge* (Duffy & Snellgrove, 1998), p. 8.
6. *OH*, p. 366.
7. E. Pentreath, *History of the 59th Battalion AIF* (59 Bn Assoc, 1968), p. 6; entry for 19 July 1916, 60 Bn WD, Item 23/77, Roll 99, AWM 4.
8. '15 Australian Infantry Brigade Report on Action 19th/20th July 1916', 23 July 1916, 15 Bde WD, Item 23/15, Roll 28, AWM 4; R.S. Corfield, *Hold Hard, Cobbers,* I, (57/60 Bn Association, 1992), p. 34; OH, p. 364.
9. Cass, 'Report on Condition of German Trenches', 22 July 1916, Appendix 32/1/15, 14 Bde WD, Item 23/14, Roll 26, AWM 4.
10. C.E.W. Bean, *Anzac to Amiens* (AWM, 1968), p. 229.
11. Entries for 19-20 July 1916, 53 Bn WD, Item 23/70, Roll 90, AWM 4, and 14 Bde WD, Item 23/14, Roll 26, AWM 4.
12. 31 Bn After Action Reports, 21 July 1916, Appendices C and D to 31 Bn WD, Item 23/48, Roll 66, AWM 4.
13. 8 Bde, 32 Bn, 'Report on Operations 19/20 July 1916', both undated: Appendix B to 8 Bde WD, Item 23/8, Roll 17, AWM 4; Appendix A to 32 Bn WD, Item 23/49, Roll 67, AWM 4.
14. Knyvett, op. cit., p.152.
15. Sloan, op. cit., p. 76; 31 Bn After Action Report (Appendix D).
16. Zander Narrative; Williams, op. cit., p. 57; Donnan to Bean, 3 February 1934, Item 12/11/5053, 2DRL/0712; Martin, op. cit; *OH*, p. 383;
17. Zander Narrative; Sloan, op. cit., p. 80.

Chapter Six

THE LONG NIGHT

On receiving word that 15 Brigade was stalled, McCay authorised Elliott at 7.45 pm to use half of his third battalion, the 58th, to reinforce the line in No Man's Land and hopefully carry it forward. Brigadier General Carter's request for support on 184 Brigade's left flank when the 61st Division renewed its attack at 9 pm reached Elliott at 8.13 pm. He tasked D and C Companies of 58 Battalion to advance through 59 Battalion against the eastern face of the Sugarloaf while 184 Brigade assaulted on the western side.

At 8.20 pm Haking was given a first hand report on the beating the 61st Division had taken. He directed Mackenzie to abort the 9 pm attack. 183 and 184 Brigades were to withdraw any men left in No Man's Land and reconstitute the front line with their respective third battalions, 2/7 Worcesters and 2/4 Ox and Bucks. Shortly afterwards, 182 Brigade advised that 2/7 Warwicks had been bombed out of the German line, eliminating the 61st Division's only toehold. 'The men who went over first are no more', Lieutenant Colonel Nutt was told. Just in time to prevent A Company 2/7 Warwicks going forward, Haking decided that all three brigades should pull back and attack again next day.[1]

In orders received at 9.10 pm, McCay was to assist Mackenzie's second attempt by ensuring that the 5th Division held onto the line it had captured. On no account, Haking said, was he to 'use additional troops in attempting to make good the unsuccessful assault on his right, but to withdraw any isolated parties from the enemy's trenches on that flank'. The artillery would then be unhampered in supporting Mackenzie in the morning. At 9.25 pm McCay informed 15 Brigade: '61st Division not attacking tonight. General Elliott may withdraw 59 Battalion and its reinforcements if he thinks attack is unlikely to succeed'. This last sentence referred to his 7.45 pm message and the use of 58 Battalion to restart 15 Brigade's advance.

Haking did not send McCay his earlier order cancelling the 9 pm attack. Carter's request to Elliott had gone via the two divisional headquarters, so Haking was probably unaware that 15 Brigade was involved. But when Mackenzie forwarded the cancellation to his brigadiers at 8.30 pm, he also advised McCay's headquarters: 'Under instructions from corps commander am withdrawing from captured enemy line after dark'. The message arrived at 8.35 pm but its meaning or its importance, or perhaps both, were overlooked and the information was not passed to Elliott. If it were, 58 Battalion's attack might have been stopped because the preparations were not completed until 8.45 pm.[2]

The End of 15 Brigade

Led by twenty-one year old Major Arthur Hutchinson, D and C Companies duly went over the parapet at 9 pm, picking up unwounded survivors of 59 Battalion as they advanced. 11 Company 3/16 BRIR waited until the Australians were two thirds of the way across No Man's Land before unleashing a torrent of fire that sounded like a thousand sheets of calico being rent at once. The line staggered, struggled on for a few steps and took cover in a shallow ditch. Seeking to inspire his men, Hutchinson rose and went on alone. Riddled by bullets, he fell on the German wire. His batman, Private Lyons, was shot trying to retrieve his body.

Back at Sailly, Haking learned that an aircraft patrol had seen flares in the Sugarloaf. Though the Germans opposing Hutchinson's attack probably fired them, he thought they came from 2/1 Bucks, which must therefore still be holding out. Cancelling his cancellation order, Haking directed Mackenzie at 11.10 pm to make 'every possible effort' to attack the Sugarloaf during the night. Lieutenant Colonel W.H Ames, whose 2/4 Ox and Bucks had taken over 184 Brigade's front line, gave the job to A and D Companies at 11.30 pm.

As before, the 5th Division would support the 61st by tying the Germans down at the captured line. But Elliott's sector on the British flank was no less important. Telling him at 10.30 pm that the Sugarloaf might be attacked again, McCay asked: 'Can you seize and hold all your objective if I give you your reserve battalion?' He was now proposing another assault, this time by 57 Battalion. Uncertain as to his situation, Elliott replied that he could not 'guarantee success of attack with 57th as enemy machine gun fire is very hot but would try'. With Haking's approval, McCay gave him half of 57 Battalion and the rest of the 58th at 11.40 pm. Together with Tivey and Pope, who were given half of their fourth battalions, the 29th and 56th, Elliott was 'to take and hold whole of original objectives'.

The likelihood of 15 Brigade assaulting for a third time evaporated forty minutes later when Elliott sent McCay a message he had just received from Major Charles Denehy, 58 Battalion's second-in-command:

...the attack of this Bde has completely failed, such men of the 60th as actually reached the enemy's trench being killed or captured, the two coys of 58th mown down when close to enemy trench and very few came back. Men of all battalions are coming back from No Man's Land...Many men are wounded, many are not. Very many officers are casualties, including Majors McCrae, Elliott and Hutchinson, all of whom are reported dead, and seems impossible to reorganise. Sapping proceeding but how long it will be possible depends on the protection provided by the others. Report seems to be unanimous to the effect that not a single man of 15 Bde is now in enemy trenches as enemy's flares are coming from the whole front allotted to the Bde. I am now organizing the defence of our original trenches and on the front Pinney's Ave and VC.[3]

At 1.10 am on 20 July, McCay told Elliott to abandon the attack and reconstitute his front line. A switch trench was to be dug to 14 Brigade's right flank but the task proved to be impossible because not even those holding it knew their precise location. The fire saturating No Man's Land ended the effort to extend Pinney's and VC Avenues. Helped by the 57th, the remnants of 58, 59 and 60 Battalions crawled in.

In 184 Brigade alongside, A and D Companies of 2/4 Ox and Bucks were filing into Rhondda Sap at 2.25 am for the attack on the Sugarloaf when the engineers said they had no stores for the consolidation. In the nick of time a message arrived from Carter telling Lieutenant Colonel Ames not to proceed unless everything was ready by 2.30 am. The assault was postponed. At 3 am Carter informed Mackenzie that his communication trenches were either smashed or full of wounded, and that the German shelling and machine gun fire were so bad as to preclude any action before daylight. Haking agreed to cancel the attack but wanted the divisional assault in the morning to go ahead.

Holding On

On the other side of No Man's Land, the German counterattacks had begun at dusk when 5 and 8 Companies from 2/21 BRIR, supported by 6 Company from that unit and 9 Company from 3/20 BRIR, struck 32 Battalion's left flank. At 8.50 pm, Toll and Coghill pleaded for more men and McCay released the rest of 30 Battalion. But its commander, Lieutenant Colonel James Clark, had used the

Lieutenant Colonel James Clark.

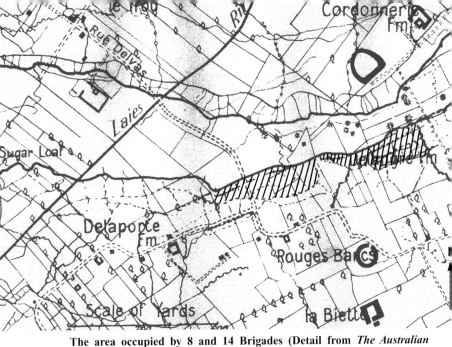

The area occupied by 8 and 14 Brigades (Detail from *The Australian Imperial Force in France 1916*, **Map 6**).

two companies, C and D, as carriers after B Company stayed on to fight. They became emmeshed in the battle too. He had few men left to send.

Captain Frank Krinks and his carrying party were drawn in when the Germans seemed about to burst out of Delangré Farm. Grabbing eleven men, he reinforced the barricade in the Kastenweg by tearing the ammunition boxes from the trench walls, but fierce bombing forced the group into some shell holes twenty yards from the eastern side of the trench. From there they could snipe at the Germans, who were silhouetted on the higher ground of the farm ruins when they shot at 32 Battalion on the western side. Realising the importance of this position, Krinks went back to Clark's headquarters in the Australian front line and returned with two Lewis guns, whose fire stymied 2/21 BRIR's attempts to drive down the Kastenweg thereafter.

Private P.J. Nankivell.

Crossing with ammunition, sandbags and tools, Lieutenant T.C. Barbour's platoon encountered a legless soldier crawling back to the breastwork on his stumps. 'Make way please', the mortally wounded man gasped as he passed, never to be seen again. Finding only dead and wounded in the posts connecting 31 and 32 Battalions, Barbour's men occupied them, and Private P.J. Nankivell reached Clark's headquarters, despite horrific injuries, with a rough sketch of the position. Next, Barbour redistributed the ammunition from the casualties to the posts engaging the Germans on the left. Along with Krinks' XI, they beat them off, the German history admitting that the companies of 21 BRIR 'lost their nerve due to the sustained barrages of the Australian machine guns and rifles'.[4]

A more dangerous situation loomed on the right flank, where Second Lieutenant Bachschneider's men had resumed their push along the German breastwork after ejecting 53 Battalion's bombers. They arrived at a communication trench to Captain Arblaster's advanced line at the same time as a thirty-man working party from 55 Battalion under Lieutenant E.M. Farmer, which was to improve the trench so that the advanced line could be accessed safely. Farmer had only two experienced bombers and unfused grenades. He fused them himself and the bombers blocked the Germans' path.

Unaware that the Germans were behind him, Arblaster was stunned to see their *picklehaubes* silhouetted against the flashes of the explosions. He sent anyone who could be spared to bomb them. After an hour of ferocious fighting, the grenades ran out and Arblaster had to pull his men back to the advanced line. Farmer's group was also swept aside. Bachschneider had retaken over 100 yards of 3/21 BRIR's front line, which the Germans now held almost to the Rue Delvas, directly opposite the site of the Australian Memorial Park. In his headquarters on the eastern side of the road, Cass did not know that they were so close or that 14 Brigade's right was partly cut off. But Lieutenant Colonel David McConaghy, the commander of 55 Battalion, did. He had landed at Gallipoli with 3 Battalion and led it through the hellish fighting at Lone Pine.

As 55 Battalion was fully committed when Captain Gibbins and Lieutenant Matthews took their companies across, McConaghy and his deputy, Major Robert Cowey, another original Anzac, followed them and set up battalion headquarters in the German front line at N.9.d.5.2, 100 yards west of Cass's position. After locating Arblaster, who did not mince words about the threat on the right, they sent out patrols that found the Germans there as far as they could see. McConaghy ordered the breastwork to be barricaded. Two blocks, covered by snipers and bombers, were thrown up and Bachschneider's thrust could make no headway against them. It ran out of

Lieutenant Colonel David McConaghy.

93

Sandbags put in place by the Australians to make a parapet at the rear of a ditch they occupied.

steam around 11 pm. Sergeant F. Law crawled out to bayonet the crew of a machine gun on the Rue Delvas near Rouges Bancs.

By now the water level in the ditches was so high that the Germans were suspected of flooding them. Any man hit while working drowned unless his mates were close enough to pull him out. Where possible, the wounded were put in the first line of *Wohngraben*. Incredibly, a breastwork of sorts was built up, including across the Rue Delvas to close the gap it made between the ditches on either side. At midnight the extension of Brompton Road finally reached the German front line behind Cass's headquarters, and Gibbins started sending carrying parties back along it. Major Henry Bachtold, the commander of 14 Engineer Company, gave a breakdown of the engineer effort:

> *Total length of the trench was 195 yards, made up of 20 yards of German sap (required clearing of barbed wire), 25 yards of an old ditch or gully in the centre of No Man's Land and 150 yards of new trench. 120 infantry and 40 sappers digging and 40 infantry carrying duckboards and bags.*[5]

Behind 8 Brigade, Captain Allen's switch trench inched across No Man's Land. German shelling often destroyed sections as soon as they were dug and, at one stage, 9 Company 3/21 BRIR launched a lightning sally that drove the diggers back to their own line. The signallers who kept 8 Brigade's telephone link intact for most of the battle – another tremendous feat – had a terrible time as well. Writing in the third person and calling himself Ted, seventeen-year old Corporal Rowland Lording of 30 Battalion was tracing a cable run out at 10 pm:

God! What sights they see out there. Huddled and stretched out bodies, khaki heaps that were once men – some of A Company digging a trench – others like themselves, making short crouching runs and flinging themselves down before anything that will afford the slightest cover.

Crump! Bang! Crash! The shells fall. Zipzipzip - zipzip! Machine-gun bullets kick up the dirt around them. A lull and they are off again. Zipzip! Bang! Another twisted heap of khaki hits the ground.

It is Ted. He does not move. His cobbers crawl over to his side. 'Where d'you get it?' they ask him. His lips move, but they do not hear his reply. His arm is shattered and blood is gushing from his side. He cannot last much longer – they think he is going west. His eyes ask them to do something. Stan rolls him on to a groundsheet and drags him yard by yard towards the trench. Shell splinters tear through the sheet. The ground rocks from a nearby shell-burst which almost covers them with mud. Stan drags him on. Ted is in mortal fear of being hit again. At last they come to the sally-port and he is carried on a duckboard into the trench.

They give him the worst possible thing. He gulps down some rum, chokes, coughs blood, loses his breath; blood bubbles from his side, he is in the throes of death. He quietens. They give him water. If they can stop the bleeding he might survive. With a bandaged lead pencil they probe back his lung and plug the wound with a field-dressing and pieces torn from a greatcoat. They fix a tourniquet and bind his arm to a piece of duckboard. This completes their rough but honest first aid.[6]

Lording lost six ribs and his right arm and underwent many more operations before dying in a mental hospital in 1944.

In the German breastwork, 31 Battalion was being hit from front and back. Machine guns in the German strongpoints fired at openings in the parados where saps entered. As parts of the parapet had been destroyed during the bombardment, the men trying to plug them were also exposed to the machine guns in the Australian front line. The sandbags were rotten and fell apart, so dead Germans were used instead. Apart from one post, the line between Lieutenant Colonel

Australian dead in the German breastwork.

Toll's left at N.10.c.3.3 and 32 Battalion's position at the head of the Kastenweg, a distance of 300 yards, was empty. The wounded were the only occupants on the other side until McConaghy's bombers were reached on the extreme right.

Towards midnight, Toll reinforced his left with a half company from 29 Battalion. Claiming 'there was no other option', Lieutenant Colonel Clark had sent A and D Companies of the 29th across by 11.35 pm, which was before McCay released the halves of the fourth battalions. As B and C Companies were garrisoning its front line, 8 Brigade had no reserve left. Except for C and D Companies of 56 Battalion in the 300 Yard Line, McCay had no troops to draw on either. The Germans, on the other hand, had committed hardly any of their reserves.[7]

The Second Counterattack

Just after 1 am, Second Lieutenant Arnold led 2/16 BRIR's composite company through the Heckengraben and into the German front line, where it relieved Bachschneider's group. 1 Company 1/16 BRIR arrived shortly afterwards, allowing the Germans on the right flank to attack along the breastwork and ditches simultaneously. As Arblaster called repeatedly for bombs and bombers, Captain Murray on the Rue Delvas motioned to one officer after another to head into the inferno with his men. Fewer than one in ten returned, and the Germans' progress was inexorable. By 3 am they were over the road and their fire into the back of the 53 Battalion's advanced line all but cut it off from 54 and 55 Battalions on the other side.

With ammunition running short, Arblaster knew that the only chance lay in charging the German front line. He distributed the last grenades, lined his men out and gave the signal. Met by a hail of fire they recoiled back into their trench. Arblaster was shot through both arms and died of septicaemia in a German military hospital in Douai on 24 July. As the survivors and the men near Murray crabbed back along the ditches to the Rue Delvas and into 54 Battalion's advanced line, cries of 'We have been ordered to retire' and 'Our own artillery are shelling us', arose. Much of what was left of 53 Battalion broke.

Pioneer Sergeant A.W. Stringer rallied a dozen shaken men and temporarily halted the Germans by hurling grenades from the parapet of the breastwork 'like cricketers throwing at a wicket', while dodging the stick bombs they tossed back. Major Cowey returned to the Australian line to scrounge reinforcements. At 4.20 pm Cass warned Pope: 'Position almost desperate' and asked for more artillery support. Pope replied that the guns could do no more than they were already doing. McCay had arranged for them to bombard both flanks and for 15 Brigade and 60 Brigade to lay down suppressive fire as the light improved.[8]

At the same time, Lieutenant W. Denoon led fifty men along the parapet and parados. Others from B Company 56 Battalion, who were improving the communication trench, joined in. They had regained eighty yards of the German front line when Cowey arrived with some of the 56th's bombers. For the next hour a massive bomb fight raged either side of the Rue Delvas. At the end of it, the Germans had taken back forty yards but were too worn out to go further. 16 BRIR's history noted, 'After twenty or thirty throws the people had always to be relieved'.[9] Private Charles Johnston was among the Australian dead.

The Germans had also lapped around the front of 53 Battalion's position but were stopped by riflemen who moved into shell holes to snipe at them. Once the 53rd had gone, their attack drove up the Rue Delvas and into a ditch that was just beyond the southern fence of the Australian Memorial Park and behind the advanced line. With no

The left flank (from 32 Battalion War Diary).

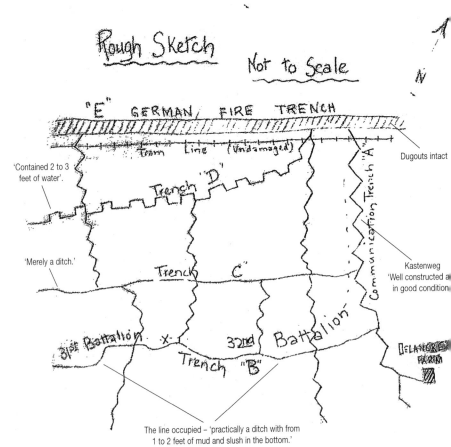

protecting parados, its occupants were now very exposed. A Lewis gunner in Lieutenant C.T. Agassiz's post rested his weapon on the shoulder of Corporal G.H. Stringfellow and fired downwards into the ditch. Agassiz took over when the gunner was shot through the head. Here, too, the attack was held, the German history mentioning the trouble this machine gun caused. But more companies from 1/16 BRIR were arriving and two companies of 17 BRIR had been made available. The morning mist covered their approach.

For 8 Brigade, though, the end was near. Advancing over the Rue Delvas east of Rouge Bancs around 2.30 am, 1/21 BRIR and two companies of 1/20 BRIR swamped B Company in 31 Battalion's screen. Captain Mills, its commander, had just returned from seeing Captain White about the ongoing build-up at Delangré Farm when a bomb shattered his right hand and a German under-officer, grabbing him, said in English, 'Why do you not put up your hands, officer? Come with me.'[10] Lieutenant Drayton's advanced post was pushed into Toll's position but Toll and A Company 55 Battalion under Captain Gibbins kept the left of the assault at bay. The right got into the German front line and tore eastwards, rolling up the men from 29

Captain Mills in German hands.

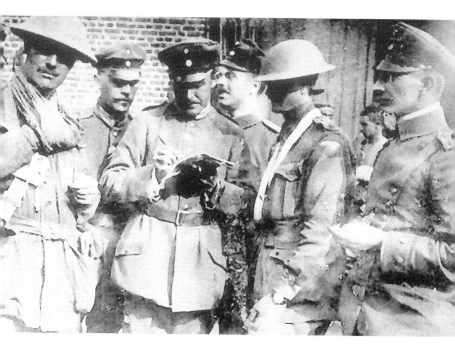

Battalion Toll had sent there and 32 Battalion's post at the Kastenweg.

At 3.15 am, Captain Kenneth Mortimer, commanding A Company 29 Battalion, told Lieutenant Mills at the Kastenweg barricades that the bombing he had heard in rear meant the Germans were behind the ditch Captain White's men held. Mortimer went off to check and was never seen again. Wounded twice, Mills had done the same job at the barricades as Arblaster on the right. He gave the news to White and both agreed that with 2/21 BRIR again breaking out of Delangré Farm ahead of them, they had no chance of driving the Germans out of the front line behind them. The only hope was a charge through it and back to the Australian line.

When the signal was given at 3.45 am, 150 men from all four 8 Brigade battalions dashed towards the German breastwork as machine guns opened up on all sides. White and many others had to fight their way over it. The machine guns at the Tadpole caused heavy losses in No Man's Land, although some men got across through the switch trench, all but twenty yards of which had been completed. Half of Krinks XI made it to the breastwork, where the Germans seized two of them. The others turned back and freed their mates with a flurry of punches. Krinks and three others reached 60 Brigade's line. Those who could not break through or did not get the retirement order fought on until they were killed or captured. Lieutenant Zander witnessed the end of a Lewis gun crew:

> *After all the rest had fallen back they could still be heard firing. We could see the Bosche working in along the trench on both their flanks toward them, but they still stuck to their post and the gun kept firing. We saw some stick bombs thrown into their little stronghold – then silence!*[11]

The splendid enfilade view of the left flank from the Tadpole.

DELANGRÉ FARM   GERMAN FRONT LINE   BRITISH FRONT L.

Toll's group was out of grenades and a brace of shells had smashed the Vickers gun at the heart of their defence when the Germans attacked again at 5.30 pm. They soon bombed through to the front line on Toll's right, cutting him off from 14 Brigade, whereupon:

At 5.45 am, the remnants of our troops broke and retired and it was impossible to restrain them although an attempt was made to keep them at the point of the revolver. The CO was the last man to leave the enemy's trench. The enemy then swarmed in and the retirement across No Man's Land resembled a shambles, the enemy artillery and machine guns doing deadly damage.[12]

The Withdrawal

At 5 am, McCay and Mackenzie had met Haking at his headquarters in Sailly to plan the 61st Division's fresh attack. Monro was also present. They had no sooner started than McCay's chief-of-staff telephoned with news from Pope that Cass's situation was critical and from Tivey that 8 Brigade was back in its own line. He wanted to know whether 14 Brigade should be reinforced or withdrawn. Monro opted to abandon the attack and withdraw. The artillery started a box barrage around the pocket at 5.40 pm to protect the retirement. Pope had warned Cass at 5.15 am that a withdrawal was likely but that he should wait for the order. Because of another breakdown at McCay's headquarters, Pope was not given the order for over an hour. He sent it to Cass at 6.30 am. But messages were taking 1½ hours to get through.

In the meantime, the rest of 1/16 BRIR had streamed through the Teufelsgraben, a strongpoint in N.15.b between Delaporte Farm and Rouge Bancs, and linked up with 1/21 BRIR's attack. The onslaught stunned Sergeant Archibald Winter of 55 Battalion:

God knows which way he came – we don't. He appeared to come from every direction. We were unsupported, consequently Fritz could come in on our own flanks. They had snipers everywhere and our own men were falling fast. Then we got into close quarters with the bombs but we were only a handful and Fritz was there in his thousands.[13]

Captain Gibbins, though wounded in the head, led several attacks along the parapet to bomb the Germans out of the line Toll had left. Receiving Pope's warning order for the withdrawal at 6.30 am, Cass directed him to form a rearguard. But stress and fatigue corrupted his instructions. Though Cass had not intended it, Gibbins immediately pulled all of his men back to the German front line, allowing the Germans to get between it and the Australian advanced line.

The withdrawal order finally reached Cass at 7.50 am – eight runners were needed to get it through. He spread the word to use the communication trench across No Man's Land, the head of which Gibbins's rearguard was holding. Many were shot down while charging towards it. Those who succeeded could only move slowly along its congested course and the rearguard was hard pressed to keep the Germans at arm's length while they got away. Cass was among the last to leave; the inspirational Gibbins was the last. Finding the trench blocked with wounded near the Australian line, he climbed out and was on the parapet when he looked back at the German line. At that instant Gibbins was shot in the head and killed. Half of his rearguard were lost.

The men of 56 Battalion saw those who could not reach the communication trench strike out across the open:

The morning after. Germans reoccupying their second line.

We were powerless to assist them, and had to watch them being shot down at point-blank range...It seemed an eternity of time until the lucky ones reached our parapets, to be pulled in by willing hands. No sooner was our field of fire clear than we blazed into the Germans who had lined their parapets to punish the retiring troops.[14]

Some with no chance of getting back surrendered. Others fought on until they were overwhelmed. The infantry action was over by 9.30 am and the artillery switched to a desultory bombardment of the German line at 10.15 am. By midday, with the gunners on both sides exhausted, the shelling ceased altogether and an uncanny stillness descended on the battlefield, broken only by the pitiful cries coming from No Man's Land.

The Wounded

'The scene in the Australian trenches, packed with wounded and dying, was unexampled in the history of the AIF', wrote Bean, and was burned into the mind of everyone who saw it. 'If you had gathered the stock of a thousand butcher-shops...it would give you a faint conception of the shambles those trenches were', Lieutenant Knyvett remembered. Not bothering with descriptive metaphors, Sergeant Martin saw 'dead bodies lying in all directions, just as they had fallen, some without heads, other bodies torn about minus arms or legs, or pieces cut clean out of them by shells'.[15]

Chaplain Spencer Maxted, who had marched with 54 Battalion from Tel-el-Kebir though entitled to ride, was killed by a shell after helping to evacuate 150 men. Elliott looked like a man 'who had just lost his wife'. He wept openly as he shook hands with what was left of 15 Brigade and assisted the wounded. Tivey, too, was 'quite overdone – with eyes like boiled gooseberries. The one thing he tried to assure himself of was that his brigade had done as well as those at Gallipoli'. 'They'll get used to it', McCay was overheard telling him.[16]

Chaplain Spencer Maxted.

While the casualties in the front line could at least be tended, the plight of the wounded in No Man's Land was heart-rending. They were thickest in front of the Australian line and 'could be seen everywhere raising their limbs in pain or turning hopelessly, hour after hour, from one side to the other'. Parched by the sun and tormented by flies and ants, they moaned for water or for an end to the agony. Unable to stand their suffering, other Australians crawled out to help. Private William Miles was looking for Captain Mortimer when an English-speaking Bavarian lieutenant beckoned and told him to come back with an Australian officer to arrange a truce to collect them.

As soldiers crowded the parapets on both sides to watch, Major Alexander Murdoch of D Company 29 Battalion returned with Miles. The Germans proposed that he remain as a hostage while each side's stretcher-bearers cleared its half of No Man's Land. Many were brought in while the truce was referred to McCay. Aware of GHQ's position on truces, he rejected it. Monro and Haking approved the decision but the men saw it as another example of McCay's callousness. They took matters into their own hands, slipping out during the next several nights – 250 were found on the night of 20/21 July alone – and, where possible,

Sergeant Simon Fraser.

during the days, to rescue their comrades. Sergeant Simon Fraser and some mates from 57 Battalion had gone out to fetch a man from near the German wire when another man called out, 'Don't forget me, cobber'. He was also recovered and his cry became part of Australian folklore.[17]

Cruelty, humanity and tragedy intermingled. Preventing all attempts to save a man who had been blinded, the Germans let him stumble in circles near the Sugarloaf for several days before they shot him. Two Germans carried a wounded Australian to his own parapet, saluted and walked away. Unaware of what had happened, other Australians shot them. Lieutenant Krinks and the three men who escaped with him went back to pick up their wounded and were returning with them when a panicky Australian sentry killed two of the rescuers with a single shot. Another Australian, hit through the arm, took food and water from the dead during the seven days it took to drag his wounded mate in. Captain Liddelow's younger brother, Roy, was badly wounded while searching for him. One man was found eight days after the attack.

The 61st Division's lines were also a spectacle of 'destruction and havoc' that was 'impossible to forget'. Often working in daylight, its battalions were still recovering wounded on 23 July. Chaplain Bennett was awarded 2/8 Warwicks' first Military Cross for his rescue efforts. The British captured the area in the last weeks of the war and, on

Father Louis Dahiez, Fromelles' postwar priest, kneels in 1919 before the remains of an English or Australian soldier killed during the battle. (M. Delebarre)

Armistice Day 1918, C.E.W. Bean revisited it:

We found the old No Man's Land simply full of our dead. In the narrow sector west of the Laies River and east of the Sugarloaf Salient, the skulls and bones and torn uniforms were lying about everywhere. I found a bit of Australian kit lying fifty yards from the corner of the salient, and the bones of an Australian officer and several men within 100 yards of it. Farther round, immediately on their flank, were a few British – you could tell them by their leather equipment. And within 100 yards of the west corner of the Sugarloaf Salient there was a small party of English too – also with an officer – you could tell from the cloth of his coat.[18]

NOTES

1. 'Report on Operations 19-7-16', 21 July 1916, 2/7 Warwicks WD.
2. Messages, 19 July, 5 Div WD, Item 1/50, Roll 836, AWM 4; *OH*, pp. 392-4.
3. Messages from entries for 19 July and Appendices: 15 Bde WD, Item 23/15, Roll 28, AWM 4; 5 Div WD, Item 1/50, Roll 836, AWM 4.
4. Corfield, op cit., pp. 186, 229.
5. Quoted in 'Fromelles Inquiry', *Journal of the Royal United Service Institution of NSW*, Vol. 50, No. 4, Summer 1997/98, p. 56.
6. R.E. Lording (aka 'A. Tiveychoc'), *There and Back* (RSL of Australia, 1935), pp. 171-3.
7. 31 Bn Report; OH, p. 414.
8. *OH*, p. 418; entry for 20 July 1916, 14 Bde WD, Item 23/14, Roll 26, AWM 4.
9. 16 BRIR History quoted in Corfield, op. cit., p. 198.
10. Ellis, op. cit., p. 104.
11. Zander Narrative.
12. 31 Bn Report.
13. Entry for 19-20 July 1916, Winter D, Item 89/15/80, 1DRL/0417, AWM.
14. Williams, op. cit., p. 62.
15. *Anzac to Amiens*, p. 235; Knyvett, op. cit., p. 155; Martin, op. cit.
16. Entry for 20 July 1916, Bean D52, 3DRL/606, AWM; Corfield, op. cit., p. 83.
17. *OH*, p. 437; Fraser to family, 31 July 1916, 1DRL/300, AWM.
18. H.T. Chidgey, *Black Square Memories* (Blackwell, 1924), p. 37; *OH*, p. 395.

Chapter Seven

REFLECTIONS

The battle had cost the 61st Division 1,547 casualties, which represented a loss rate in the assault battalions of 46 percent. As nearly all of the 5th Australian Division had been sucked in, its casualties amounted to 5,533 men. The loss rate in its assault battalions averaged 76 percent, while the flanking battalions suffered over 80 percent casualties. Of the 481 men taken prisoner, about 400 were Australian and the Germans paraded them through Lille to demoralize its French population. Only at Bullecourt in April 1917 were more Australians captured in a single battle. Casualties in the 6th BR Division totalled 1,582, of which 17 BRIR lost 274 men against the British attack, 21 BRIR 775 men against the Australians and 16 BRIR 377 men against both.[1]

From the German standpoint, the result was outstanding, and not just because of the highly favourable casualty ratio. Searching the dead

The Germans remove Australian and British dead for burial.

Australian prisoners being marched through La Bassée. Some wear slouch hats.

and the prisoners, they found a copy of the general order from Haking that was read to all troops on the eve of the assault. By stating quite plainly that the objective was 'strictly limited to the enemy's support trenches and no more', it told them that a feint had been intended. They could now move troops from the Aubers/Fromelles area to the Somme or anywhere else, defeating the whole purpose of the operation.

Reasons Why

Haking thought that the Australians attacked in 'an exceptionally gallant manner', remarked that the 61st Division 'was not sufficiently imbued with the offensive spirit to go in like one man', and blamed the reverse on the inexperience of both. 'With two trained divisions,' he said, 'the position would have been a gift after the artillery bombardment'. True, inexperience did play a part. Lieutenant Colonel McConaghy singled out many Australians' lack of familiarity with grenades: 'I even saw men throwing Mills Grenades without withdrawing the safety pin. This was not peculiar to any one Battalion'.[2]

Conversely, the German artillery and the Sugarloaf machine guns would have cut up battle-hardened troops as well. Shells and bullets do not distinguish between veteran and novice, a point made the previous year when three tested divisions were shattered in the attack on Aubers Ridge. One of them, the 8th Division, assaulted over the same frontage and the same ground as the 5th Australian Division. Indeed, the two battles were so similar as to make Fromelles a re-run of Aubers Ridge on a smaller scale. In the 1915 battle, the Germans lost 1,551 men and the three British divisions principally involved 11,279, proportionally the same as their two divisions in 1916.

If the chances of success in May 1915 were nil, what is to be said of the prospects in July 1916? Using the attack as an example of how not to do things, Sir Basil Liddell Hart decried it as 'the final link of an almost incredibly muddled chain of causation'. The planning process at the start was a dog's breakfast that Bean described in one of the most famous passages in the Australian Official History:

> *Suggested first by Haking as a feint attack; then by Plumer as part of a victorious advance; rejected by Monro in favour of attack elsewhere; put forward again by GHQ as a 'purely artillery' demonstration; ordered as a demonstration but with an infantry operation added, according to Haking's plan and through his emphatic advocacy; almost cancelled – through weather and the doubts of GHQ – and finally reinstated by Haig, apparently as an urgent demonstration – such were the changes of form through which the plans of this ill-fated operation had successively passed.*[3]

The preparations had to be rushed and were mostly undertaken by the assault units, leaving them exhausted and without the time for the rehearsals that should be carried out before any operation but which, for inexperienced troops, are vital. At least half of the Australians were yet to be issued with helmets, which accounts for their high proportion of head wounds.

Behind the British lines, the attack was common knowledge to the extent that French civilians knew the details. Even if word did not drift back to the Germans, they had a grandstand view from Aubers Ridge of the activity below them. Their artillery was thus able to do tremendous damage even though it had far fewer guns.

As was the case at Aubers Ridge, dropshorts from the friendly artillery caused many casualties. In another reminder of the 1915 battle, both Mackenzie and McCay commented that, apart from the sectors attacked by 182 Brigade and 8 Brigade, the German line was undamaged. Of the seventy-five concrete shelters 16 BRIR had built into the breastwork facing 184 and 15 Brigades, the shelling destroyed eight, damaged seven and missed sixty. 2/1 Bucks pointed to the way the Germans manned their line as complicating the artillery's task:

> *One of the most striking lessons to be learnt from the attack is that the very greatly superior method of holding trenches adopted by the Germans should at once be followed. Whereas on our Battalion front, the Regiment had NOT ONE bomb proof*

shelter and lost 100 casualties from shelling alone, the Germans appeared to have about six teams of Machine Gunners, and very few infantry, and even after seven hours of bombardment by our guns, these six teams of machine gunners appeared intact – firing over the parapet at our assaulting infantry. By crowding three companies into three hundred yards of front, our casualties from shellfire were the more heavy.[4]

The Germans also manned their front line observation posts throughout the bombardment, regardless of casualties. 16 BRIR's history lavished praise on these lookouts, whose courage ensured that the garrison was at the parapet as soon as it lifted:

Whenever someone was wounded or shot another took his place against the breastworks, staring with burning eyes through the smoke and dust of the fiery explosions to the greyish brown stripe of the enemy position in order not to miss the moment when the English would first commence their attack. Every man who loyally watched in this firestorm was at that time the personification of the German Army on the Western Front.[5]

The battalions that entered the German line had to contend with lightning counter-penetrations, a trademark skill that won the Germans the admiration of their opponents in both world wars. Having dealt with 60 Battalion, for example, 10 Company of 3/16 BRIR under Second Lieutenant Bachschneider hooked into 53 Battalion, which had

The executioners. A German machine gun crew.

109

overrun 3/21 BRIR's right. Some of 3/21 BRIR's survivors helped the garrison at Delangré Farm pin down 32 Battalion. Their actions gained time for the rehearsed move from the Aubers Ridge area of the support and reserve battalions that would counterattack. Lieutenant Colonel Nutt, whose 2/7 Warwicks was the only British battalion to gain a lodgement, considered that the Germans mustered sufficient strength quickly enough to preclude holding on even if the neighbouring 2/6 Warwicks had taken their objective.

All things considered, it is difficult to see how the attack could have succeeded, a conclusion the British Official Historian reached in his summing up:

> To have delivered battle at all, after hurried preparation, with troops of all arms handicapped by their lack of experience and training in offensive trench-warfare, betrayed a grave under-estimate of the enemy's powers of resistance. The utmost endeavours of the artillery were unable either to subdue the German batteries or to 'reduce the defenders to a state of collapse before the assault', so the infantry, advancing in broad daylight, paid the price. Even if the German defences had been completely shattered by the British bombardment, and the infantry assault had succeeded, it would probably have proved impossible to hold the objective under the concentrated fire of the enemy's artillery directed by excellent observation.

Though they have favourably re-interpreted many of the BEF's operations on the Western Front, modern British military historians do not disagree. 'We assure you that not all the Brits were quite as stupid as that', the Imperial War Museum's Peter Simkins remarked during a discussion on Fromelles with some Australian historians in 1998. 'This is one of the areas where we're pretty indefensible, I think'.[6]

Recriminations

The Australians, wrote Sergeant Williams, felt they had been 'sacrificed on the altar of incompetence'. Elliott blamed Haking, accusing him of learning nothing from the failure at the Boar's Head a few weeks earlier. A more valid point was that he had commanded the 1st Division at Aubers Ridge over a year earlier and knew better than anyone what to expect.[7]

A passionate believer in the offensive, Haking was irrepressible in urging the attack and had even wanted to press on to Aubers Ridge. Despite knowing that much of it was untried, he placed great faith in the artillery, while the divisional boundary he set maximised the influence of the Sugarloaf. To say afterwards, as Haking did, 'The artillery preparation was adequate . . . The wire was properly cut, and the assaulting battalions had a clear run into the enemy's trenches', was patently false. Reprising his comment after the 39th Division lost heavily at the Boar's Head, he claimed that the operation had 'done both Divisions a great deal of good', as though massive casualties made a formation proficient. 'Haking was always "Butcher Haking" after this battle', wrote Phillip Landon, 182 Brigade's staff captain. Its commander, Brigadier General Gordon, thought the attack was hopeless. In April 1918 Haking figured prominently in a War Cabinet discussion of officers judged to be incompetent.[8]

When Bean was writing the Australian Official History after the war, his British counterpart, Brigadier General Sir James Edmonds, tried to defend Haking by alluding to his highly regarded prewar writings and, ironically, the 'great distinction' he earned while commanding the 1st Division in 1915. Edmonds also sent him the drafts of Bean's Fromelles chapters in September 1927. After nine months of silence, Haking said that he had no wish to say anything. In a classic about turn, Edmonds confessed to Bean, 'I don't think he was much good . . . after his wound in 1914'.[9]

Although the Army Commander, General Monro, prevented another calamity by shutting the battle down before the 61st Division renewed its assault, he did not come out of it well either. Monro had reluctantly

The apex of the Sugarloaf at war's end. A line of stunted trees indicates the Laies, which 15 Brigade crossed. (M. Delebarre)

allowed himself to be carried along by Haking's enthusiasm at Aubers Ridge in 1915 and knew at first hand the ground and the strength of the German defences in 1916. But he bent with the wind again after initially rejecting Haking's proposal for the Fromelles attack. When General Butler passed on GHQ's reservations later, Monro, like Haking, insisted that it proceed. Yes, he tried to cancel the operation after the weather broke on 17 July, only for GHQ to state that it should go ahead but, even then, Haig gave him a final opportunity to call it off. As the distinguished soldier-scholar, General Sir Anthony Farrar-Hockley, remarked, 'he lacked the moral courage to do so'.[10]

Except as part of the British command responsible for the battle, Monro was too far removed for the Australians to criticise directly, as some of them did Haking. But all of them lambasted McCay. In their eyes, his insensitive comments afterwards confirmed the reputation for callous indifference he had acquired at Gallipoli and on the desert march. Henceforth, McCay, like Haking, became the 'Butcher of Fromelles'. His headquarters staff was unwilling to work for him. As a result of soldiers' letters home, he became the villain in Australia as well.

McCay's defenders insisted that he was a victim of orders he could not realistically refuse. Yet there is no evidence that he harboured any doubts about the efficacy of the attack, and he was desperately keen for his division to take part. Elliott, who did express his concerns, thought McCay should have protested. In a similar situation on the Somme on 18 July 1916, General Gough, commander of the Reserve Army, told Major General Harold Walker of the 1st Australian Division at their first meeting, 'I want you to go into the line and attack Pozières tomorrow night'. Walker, a British general, told Gough exactly what he thought and the attack was postponed. McCay might have done the same. He was, after all, a troublesome subordinate, known for arguing with his superiors. If nothing else, his qualms would have been on the record.[11]

Moreover, McCay's planning and handling of the battle were shaky. As they had done against the 8th Division in 1915, the Germans pressed against the flanks of the Australian pocket to pinch it out. McCay's order to hold only the furthest line captured was tailor-made to assist because it left the Australians without any depth and gave the Germans a free run along the breastwork behind them. In another costly error, Mackenzie's 8.35 pm message advising that the 61st Division would not be attacking again at 9 pm was overlooked. Had it been passed on to Elliott, he could have stopped 58 Battalion's suicidally hopeless charge. The omission rested with McCay and he was very anxious about it.

In December 1916 McCay left for England with severe neuritis in his wounded leg and took over the AIF training depots on Salisbury Plain. When rumours circulated eighteen months later that Birdwood would be handing over command of the Australian Corps to Monash, McCay asked for Monash's 3rd Division. Birdwood later remarked: 'I told him I didn't want the 3rd Division ruined like he had ruined the 5th!' His fellow generals threatened revolt if he were given the administrative command of the AIF instead. After the war, Australian veterans scrawled 'Butcher McCay' in red paint outside a servicemen's club he was visiting, and one of the AIF's great heroes, Captain Albert Jacka VC, MC, publicly refused to shake his hand.[12]

In yet another controversy involving McCay, Colonel Pope was sent back to Australia. The pair had never got on and when McCay was unable to rouse him on the afternoon of 20 July, he accused Pope of drunkenness and relieved him of command of 14 Brigade. Those who saw Pope at the time were divided on his condition but he insisted that he had been utterly exhausted and demanded a court martial to clear the air. Birdwood refused to grant it. Pope eventually returned to France and was given command of 52 Battalion, which he led until invalided home in February 1918. Lieutenant Colonel Cass had gone back a year earlier, his health broken by the strain of the battle and the

The German breastwork after the attack. Blankets cover the Australian dead. (M. Delebarre)

Australian and British prisoners marching through Haubordin en route to Lille. (J-M. Bailleul)

severe wounds he had sustained at Gallipoli.

On the British side, Brigadier General Carter was sacked for 184 Brigade's failure to take the Sugarloaf. Although they felt sorry for him as a scapegoat, wrote Christie-Miller, 'the Brigade were heartily glad to be rid of a commander in whom they had no confidence [and] who demonstrated daily his ignorance of the requirements of war'. But 2/1 Bucks felt deeply the dismissal of Lieutenant Colonel Williams, who had tried to point out to the disbelieving Carter that his shattered battalion was incapable of attacking the Sugarloaf again. Another plain speaker, Lieutenant Colonel Ames of 2/4 Oxfords, was also jettisoned.[13]

The finger-pointing was not just directed at the commanders. Contrasting the 1,000 yards of German line they had taken and held for over twelve hours with the almost total failure of the 61st Division, the Australians felt badly let down. As far as they were concerned, the battle confirmed the impression formed during the Gallipoli campaign that the new British divisions were not up to a tough fight. In the case of the 61st, others thought the same. At a press briefing, 'The 1st Army told the correspondents that the Australians did quite well and would have held on if 61st Division had done so. The 61st Division, they said, were rather second-rate territorials'. Disparaged by its own high command, the 61st may have believed it. By 1918, the division 'reckoned it had been unlucky at everything it had attempted and called itself the Sixty-worst'.[14]

Whether it was or not was immaterial. Like Thiepval's attackers on 1 July 1916, the 61st Division faced a task that could have only been carried out by bullet-proof men. 184 Brigade's attack foundered because No Man's Land was so wide in front of it, the same reason 15 Brigade failed. On the flanks, 182 Brigade had to go almost three times as far as 8 Brigade. In a damning lecture on the battle in 1929, Elliott attached no blame to the 61st Division. Nor could the gallantry of officers like Captains Church and Donaldson be faulted.

The Australians were also angered by the official communiqué, which described the operation as 'some important raids' to conceal the severity of the reverse. Notwithstanding this purpose, Bean questioned 'the good of deliberate lying like that', because the scale of the casualties and the loss of over 400 men as prisoners made the truth obvious. The Australian public saw through it as soon as the facts were known and from then on British official statements, which had usually been accepted at face value, were treated with great scepticism.[15]

A Question of Survival

Set against the stalemate at Verdun and the arm wrestle on the Somme, the success at Fromelles came as a welcome fillip for the Germans and they turned it into a major victory. In the 1930s the battle acquired 'a cultural relevance quite disproportionate to its military significance' on account of Hitler's involvement. Starting with the history of the List Regiment, which treated 19 July 1916 as its day of glory, each account outdid the last as the Hitler industry cashed in. On 26 June 1940, following the fall of France, Hitler himself visited Fromelles and his billet at Fournes during a two-day tour of the Flanders battlefield with two old comrades. Film captured by the Americans shows him at the N.16.c.1.1 blockhouse, pointing out hits on the side that faced the Australians.[16]

Classified as a subsidiary action by Edmonds, Fromelles was more

Hitler returns to one of his old haunts at Fromelles, 26 June 1940.   **Pointing out damage.**

or less forgotten by the British. But it remained significant for the Australians, whose '19th of July men' commemorated it annually. Their last major gathering was on the fiftieth anniversary in 1966, after which the memory faded until the Australian Memorial Park project rekindled it thirty years later. In November 1997 the Royal United Service Institution of New South Wales held an 'inquiry' into every aspect of the battle. Like all other accounts, its report makes sad reading. The courage and endurance of the men who went over the top and fought through that grim night shines through as the only redeeming feature. As one of their number, Private Jim Cleworth, recalled many years ago:

The novelty of being a soldier wore off in about five seconds, from that point on it was a question of survival. Fromelles was confusion at its best, it was like a bloody butcher's shop, it was terrible.[17]

NOTES

1. *OH*, p. 442.
2. XI Corps Report, 24 July 1916, Item 1/22/1, AWM 4; 55 Bn Report, 23 July 1916, Appendix 32/1/15 to 14 Bde WD, Item 32/14, Roll 26, AWM 4.
3. B.H. Liddell Hart, *History of the First World War* (Cassell, 1970), p. 325; *OH*, p. 350.
4. Entry for 19 July 1916, 2/1 Bucks WD, WO 95/3066, PRO.
5. Corfield, op. cit., p. 196; 'German Records Relative to Australian Operations on the Western Front', compiled by Captain J.J. Herbertson, (Class No. 111.050), AWM.
6. *Military Operations: France and Belgium, 1916. II.* p. 134; P. Simkins, *Brothers in Arms* (ABC-TV documentary, 9 November 1998).
7. Williams, op. cit., p. 68; Elliott to Bean, 15 May 1929, Elliott Papers, 3DRL/3856, AWM.
8. XI Corps Report; Travers, op. cit., p. 30; Bristow, op. cit., p. 177.
9. Edmonds to Bean, 19 September, 3 November 1927, 3 July 1928, Bean Papers, 3DRL/7953, Item 34, AWM.
10. A.H. Farrar-Hockley, *Somme* (Pan, 1983), p. 200.
11. P.A. Pedersen, 'The AIF on the Western Front' in *Australia in Two Centuries of War and Peace* (AWM, 1988), pp. 172-3.
12. P.A. Pedersen, *Monash as Military Commander* (MUP, 1992), p. 215.
13. Christie-Miller, op. cit., pp. 189-90.
14. Bean, D52, 20 July, 1916, 3DRL/606, AWM; M. Middlebrook, *The Kaiser's Battle* (Allen Lane, 1978), p. 92.
15. P. Charlton, *Pozières* (Methuen, 1986), p.116.
16. J.F. Williams, 'Words on a Lively Skirmish' in *Journal of the Australian War Memorial*, No.23, October, 1998, p. 27; *After The Battle*, No. 117, pp. 24-30.
17. Quoted in R. Austin, *Black and Gold. The History of the 29th Battalion AIF 1915-18* (Slouch Hat Publications, 1997), p. 37.

Chapter Eight

CEMETERIES AND MEMORIALS

The British and Australian dead of Fromelles and Aubers Ridge lie in cemeteries close to the old British line, on the fringes of Sailly, Laventie and Fleurbaix and on the ridge itself. Gathered into cemeteries further from the battlefield, the German dead rest at Fournes-en-Weppes, Wicres and Beaucamps.

Most of the memorials are further still. The Ploegsteert Memorial, where Captains Coulton and Wathes of 2/6 Warwicks, Bethell and Donaldson of 2/7 Warwicks and Lieutenant Kennedy of the Rifle Brigade are all commemorated, is five kilometres north of Armentières on the N365. Captain Byers of 2/4 Glosters is remembered on the Thiepval Memorial on the Somme. Nearly all of the missing from the Aubers Ridge battle are listed on the Le Touret Memorial, nine kilometres west of Fauquissart on the D171. The Loos Memorial at Dud Corner Cemetery, which is on the N43 five kilometres northwest of Lens, bears the names of 330 British missing from Fromelles.

Anzac Cemetery

On the D945 about a kilometre southwest of Sailly, Anzac Cemetery was begun by 2 Australian Field Ambulance near the site of an advanced dressing station just before the Fromelles attack and remained in use until the Germans overran the area during the Battle of the Lys in April 1918. They interred British dead in the cemetery during the summer. Of the 300 plus burials, 111 are Australian and they include many Fromelles fallen, especially from 31 Battalion. Captain Norman Gibbins, one of the heroes of the battle, rests at I.A.5. Another nineteen Australians lie in Sailly-sur-la-Lys Canadian Cemetery across the road.

The grave of Captain Norman Gibbins.

Aubers Ridge British Cemetery

As the Germans held the ridge until the

Aubers Ridge British Cemetery.

last days of the war, this cemetery was established after the Armistice to concentrate the dead from smaller cemeteries nearby and from the battlefields around Aubers. It contains burials from the 1914 battles, Neuve Chapelle and Festubert in addition to those of Aubers Ridge and Fromelles. Of the 718 graves, 445 are unknowns.

Most of the Fromelles dead were picked up from where they had fallen. Plot I consists almost entirely of 108 unidentified Australians. Another 16 Australians are named, 14 of whom belonged to 59 Battalion, which was on the right of the 5th Division's line and hence closer to Aubers than the other Australian battalions. The unknown dead from the 61st Division are concentrated in Plot II. Resting at VI.B.9, Captain William Simms of 2/6 Warwicks is among the thirty-one identified British soldiers in the cemetery, which is on the D41 750 metres south of Aubers.

Laventie Military Cemetery

Laventie and its surrounds were the principal headquarters and billeting locations for the 61st Division, which started this cemetery in June 1916. Except for when the Germans occupied the area between April-September 1918, it was continuously used, especially by the Portuguese Corps. After the war, it received the dead from several local communal and church graveyards but the 176 Portuguese fallen were removed to the Richebourg-l'Avoue Portuguese National Cemetery, leaving 417 burials.

The cemetery contains more known British dead from the Fromelles attack than any other. They are mostly from 184 Brigade and include Lieutenant Colonel Beer, the commanding officer of 2/4 Berks, at II.E.17, and Captain Church of 2/1 Bucks, who fell at the Sugarloaf, at II.E.23. Four Australians also lie at Laventie, which is

200 metres down the minor road that crosses the D166 a kilometre northeast of the town.

Le Trou Aid Post Cemetery

Shaded by poplars and willows and surrounded by a natural moat, this cemetery is literally an island of tranquillity on the Rue Petillon near its junction with the Rue Delvas. It was begun in October 1914 to serve Le Trou Aid Post, which had been set up in the 300 Yard Line at the start of Pinney's Avenue on the other side of the road.

Used until July 1915 and perhaps again in November 1916, Le Trou held 123 graves at the Armistice but was enlarged afterwards by burials from several small cemeteries to the east, most notably La Haute Loge British Cemetery in le Maisnil. It now contains 356 graves and is closely linked to the Fromelles attack. Most of the 207 unknowns, 155 British and fifty-two Australian, were probably killed during the battle. Brigadier General Lowry Cole, who died leading 25 Brigade, is among the Aubers Ridge fallen. He rests at E22.

The grave of Lieutenant Colonel John Beer. (M. Delebarre)

Le Trou Aid Post Cemetery.

Ration Farm Military Cemetery

On the D222 a kilometre northeast of Bois Grenier, this cemetery was started in October 1915 opposite Ration Farm, so-called because rations were distributed from it to the front line a kilometre eastwards. The ration parties dropped the dead off at the cemetery on their return. Remaining in use until October 1918, it was greatly expanded after the Armistice by the dead from isolated graves and small cemeteries on neighbouring battlefields. Of the 1,312 Commonwealth burials, 575 were British. Many Fromelles fallen number among the 260 Australians, 142 of them unknown, who rest together in Plots VI, VII and VIII. Major Higgon, the British regular attached to 32 Battalion, sleeps at VIII.C.15.

Rue-David Military Cemetery

Begun in December 1914, Rue-David held 220 burials when it closed three years later. Like most of the other cemeteries in the area today, it became a postwar concentration cemetery, accommodating over 650 graves from the neighbourhoods of Aubers, Fromelles and Fleurbaix. Many were of British and Australians killed on 19-20 July 1916. Almost half of the 893 burials are unidentified. The proportion is even higher for the Australians, 256 of whose 353 dead are unknowns thought to be from the battle. Resting at II.E.44, Private Billy Ellsdale was probably the first Aboriginal soldier killed in France. He died on 7 July 1916. The cemetery is located on Rue des Davids about a kilometre north of la Boutillerie.

Rue-du-Bois Military Cemetery

Many Fromelles fallen rest in this cemetery, which is on the Rue du Bois half a kilometre northeast of the Petillon crossroads. Used from 1914 to 1916 and again in 1918, except when the Germans held the area between April and September, the original cemetery comprised the current Plot I and Rows A and B of Plot II. Most of the graves are of Australians from 15 Brigade, Row B of Plot I containing twenty-seven men, and Row A of Plot II consisting of two trench graves, one believed to hold twenty-two more Australians and the other fifty-two men from 2/1 Bucks, all of whom were killed on 19-20 July 1916.

After receiving dead from the battlefields, and graveyards in Tilleloy, Picantin and Laventie in its postwar concentration role, the cemetery held 832 graves, of which 585 were British and 242 Australian. Curiously, only twenty-seven of the Australians are unknown. Major McCrae, killed after going over the top while in command of 60

Battalion, lies at I.F.33. His body was found by one of the parties recovering the wounded from No Man's Land.

Rue-Petillon Military Cemetery

Along with Le Trou, Rue-Petillon is one of the most beautiful of the local cemeteries, with entrance portals and grounds enhanced by weeping willows, mountain ash and other trees. Named after the road on which it is located at the opposite end to Le Trou and about 200 metres east of the start of Cellar Farm Avenue, it was begun in December 1914 next to the dressing station at Eaton Hall and consisted of twelve battalion burial grounds when the Germans captured the sector in April 1918. After the Armistice, concentrations from a wide area, but especially around Fleurbaix, raised the number of burials to over 1,500, about half of which were known.

British dead account for 1,129 graves and Australian for 291. Thirty men from 58 Battalion, who were killed in 1/21 BRIR's raid on 15 July, are buried in a trench grave in Row K of Plot 1. Row L has twenty-three Fromelles dead from 31 Battalion. Second Lieutenant Tenbosch of 8 Field Engineer Company and Sergeant Garland of 30 Battalion, both of whom fell while starting the switch trench, lie at I.K.3 and I.K.55 respectively. Chaplain Maxted of 54 Battalion, killed while stretcher-bearing, is next to Tenbosch at I.K.2. Perhaps the last to be buried in Rue-Petillon was Major Harrison, 54 Battalion's second-in-command. His remains were found in 1927 and identified by his silver cigarette case. He rests at I.D.20.

Rue-Petillon Military Cemetery.

VC Corner Australian Cemetery Memorial

Established after the Armistice on the Rue Delvas in the old No Man's Land crossed by 14 Brigade, VC Corner is the only all-Australian cemetery on the Western Front and, uniquely, contains no headstones. As none of the remains of the 410 Fromelles dead collected around it in 1918-19 could be identified, they were interred in two areas, each marked by a flat white cross, either side of a central grass avenue. The names of all 1,299 Australian fallen with no known grave grace a screen wall memorial at the rear. They include Lieutenant Colonel Norris and Major Sampson of 53 Battalion; Major Elliott, 60 Battalion's second-in-command; Private Weakley of 31 Battalion; Second Lieutenant Lees from 30 Battalion; and Private Charles Johnston of 56 Battalion. Services are held annually at the cemetery on Anzac Day, 19 July and 11 November. The hornbeams at the front can be seen from every part of the battlefield.

Private Charles Johnston commemorated at VC Corner Australian Cemetery Memorial.

VC Corner Australian Cemetery Memorial.

The Kennedy Crucifix

Lieutenant Paul Kennedy, a company commander in 2/Rifle Brigade, was one of the three sons of Sir John Kennedy, a senior diplomat, who fell in the war. As well as being officially commemorated on the Ploegsteert Memorial, he is remembered by this private memorial, which stands opposite Rouge Bancs on the Rue Delvas at N.15.b.7.7. It marks the area reached by his battalion on 9 May 1915 and has a poignant history.

The Kennedy Crucifix.

In 1921, Lady Kennedy, accompanied by her daughter and Leo, the surviving son, visited Fromelles with a crucifix carved in Austria that she wanted to set up as a memorial to Paul. It was duly erected and dedicated not just to him but to his three subaltern friends, Talbot Stanhope, the younger son of the Earl of Harrington, Henry Hardinge, the eldest son of Lord and Lady Hardinge and a nephew of the Viceroy of India, and Edward Leigh, the only son of Sir Chandos Leigh, together with all those who fell in the attack on Aubers Ridge.

Leo Kennedy returned to Fromelles with his daughter Clare in 1955 to find the memorial enclosed within a fence and, following an earlier collapse, re-erected on a plinth of bricks taken from German blockhouses. Both he and the local priest agreed that it symbolised the tremendous losses of the First World War and should be preserved in the church. Clare unveiled the replacement crucifix after it was installed. The ASBF cares for the memorial now.

The Australian Memorial Park

Located on the site of the German front line where it struck the eastern side of the Rue Delvas, this memorial is one of the most evocative on the old Western Front. Its origins were linked to Australian historian John Laffin's long campaign for a memorial to the Australian Corps at Hamel on the Somme. Laffin felt that the memorials to the Canadians on Vimy Ridge, the Newfoundlanders at Beaumont-Hamel and the South Africans at Delville Wood were embarrassing reminders that Australia had nothing comparable to commemorate the war service and sacrifice of its own soldiers. In 1992, Air Vice-Marshal Alan Heggen, the Director of the Office of Australian War Graves, took up the Hamel project, which would commemorate an Australian feat of arms, but he was also drawn by the idea of a memorial at Fromelles, where the devotion of men to their wounded and dying mates represented the triumph of the Australian spirit.

M. Francis DeLattre, the mayor of Fromelles, was enthusiastic and Mme Anne-Marie Descamps-Carré offered to donate the land, on which some German blockhouses still stood. Heggen hoped to have the memorial ready for the eightieth anniversary in 1996 but funding priorities caused a two-year delay. The Australian Minister of Veterans' Affairs, Bruce Scott, and M. Alain Ohrel, *Prefet* of the Nord, finally unveiled it and opened the park on 5 July 1998, the day after the dedication of the memorial park at Hamel.

As at Hamel, information panels explain the battle. But the centrepiece at Fromelles is unique, a 2.1 metre bronze statue by Melbourne sculptor Peter Corlett. In keeping with Heggen's original vision, it is based on the incident on 20 July in which Sergeant Simon Fraser responded to a wounded soldier's cry, 'Don't forget me, Cobber'. Corlett had earlier sculpted the Bullecourt Digger, which crowns the battlefield on which Fraser fell in May 1917.

Cobbers.

'Cobbers', as it is officially known, depicts a soldier from 57 Battalion, whom Corlett modelled on Fraser, carrying a wounded mate from 60 Battalion over his shoulder. In what might be seen as an unrealistic touch, the cobber, Australian slang for mate, clings tightly to his slouch hat. But his action unmistakeably identifies where the men are from and hence the memory they are clinging to as they head towards their line. On the way, they will pass VC Corner, where 410 of their cobbers are buried and over 800 more are remembered.

The Australian Memorial Park.

Chapter Nine

BATTLEFIELD TOURS

Interpreting the Fromelles battlefield is easy as long as several things are kept in mind. Because it is so flat, good vantage points are non-existent. The area around Fromelles church offers useful views but is well outside the battle area. Remember that the Rue Delvas ran diagonally across the axis of the Australian assault until it passed VC Corner Cemetery, which is in No Man's Land and *not* the Australian front line. Of the 700 blockhouses the Germans built in the area, 96 survive but many postdate the battle. Road names often change. The Rue du Bois becomes the Rue de Tilleloy and the Rue Delvas also has several aliases.

On the plus side, landmarks that can serve as reference points to key sites abound. None is more useful than the hornbeams in VC Corner Cemetery. They are visible from most parts of the battlefield, which makes the cemetery an excellent orientation point and allows the position of the Rue Delvas and the two front lines to be estimated from a long way away. So little has changed that if the modern IGN maps were appropriately marked up, they could pass as the old trench maps. Walking or cycling is a doddle, even on the hottest of summer days. The flatness does have its advantages!

Cobbers

On the eastern shoulder of the Rue Delvas at N.9.d.4.1, the Australian Memorial Park is the most important location within the battle area. It stands on a stretch of the German front line that was manned by 3/21 BRIR, and around which the heaviest fighting took place. Most of the other key sites can be identified from it, while the Cobbers statue and the park's proximity to VC Corner Cemetery mean that it is recognisable from most of them. Held by 3/16 BRIR in May 1915, it was also at the centre of the 8th Division's attack. Given its overall significance and its central role in any tour, a description of the park and the battlefield as seen from it would seem appropriate at the outset. Parking is no problem.

Looking northwards, VC Corner Cemetery is 200 metres along the Rue Delvas. Broken by farm buildings, the distant tree line to its right follows the Rue Petillon. The Rue du Bois – the D171 – extends across the horizon to its left. Overlooked by the needle-like spire of Laventie church further north, this road goes through Picantin and Tilleloy to Fauquissart, whose squat church steeple rises almost due west. The 61st Division's line began there and roughly parallelled the nearer side of the D171 until it swung eastwards below Laventie church, where the Australians took over. Crossing the Rue Delvas 250 metres beyond VC Corner Cemetery, their line passed by Cellar Farm, which is the long house facing the park 750 metres away, and brushed the left side of the prominent copse to the northeast.

The tree line to the left of the copse masks Cordonnerie Farm, Delangré Farm is behind the tall, thickish growth to the right of the copse and the telegraph poles in between track the German line towards the park. A clump of bush eastwards hides the next two blockhouses comprising it. In the opposite direction, the German line headed west to the Sugarloaf, whose apex was in the fields 720 metres from the park in N.8.d. Unfortunately, no convenient reference point exists to indicate its position. But all is not lost!

About 130 metres south of your location, the Rue Deleval runs southwest from an old corner café to meet the Rue d'Enfer (D41). The first house after the café is Delaporte Farm, site of a major strongpoint, and the next, a long white building, is La Ferme Equestre L'Hippocrate, which the British called Orchard House. Draw an imaginary line northwards from it, and the intersection with another line running west from the park is the approximate location of the Sugarloaf. Easy!

Now look south. The Kennedy Crucifix is 220 metres away on the sharp bend that carries the road eastwards past Rouge Bancs. If the fields have been harvested, the blockhouse at N.16.c.1.1, where Hitler possibly sheltered, can be discerned to the right of the crucifix roughly a kilometre further on. The ground behind rises to Aubers Ridge. Although the wooded slope conceals Aubers, Fromelles church is visible on the southwestern skyline.

Note the narrowness of No Man's Land east of the park compared to its width westwards. It was 220 metres across at the park, where the breastwork ran just beyond the fence on the northern side. Attacking on the left of the Rue Delvas, 53 Battalion was badly enfiladed from

The attack by 14 and 8 Brigades as seen from the Australian Memorial Park.

RUE DELVAS   VC CORNER AUSTRALIAN CEMETERY MEMORIAL   LE TROU AID POST   14 BRIGA

the Sugarloaf, before which 184 and 15 Brigades had been shot down. A machine gun, possibly 'Parapet Joe', firing down the road from the entrance to the park, was also troublesome. When Lieutenant Colonel Norris was killed on the breastwork, Captain Arblaster took command. They were in the supporting waves, which ejected 12 Company 3/21 BRIR.

After an easy crossing, 54 Battalion alongside overran 11 Company, which it caught coming out of shelters in the breastwork and *Wohngraben* in rear. They were subsequently used to shelter the wounded. The deepest *Wohngraben* were strung out behind the line of concrete blockhouses in the park. Advancing over them and the light tramway that ran along the far side of the southern fence, the assault went as far as Rouge Bancs, while 53 Battalion on the right crossed the Rue Deleval. Some men went on towards the blockhouse at N.16.c.1.1. Unable to find a clearly defined trench in the grass, both battalions returned to some watery ditches in the fields south of the park, which were the remains of the second and third lines they had been seeking.

The 53rd held a line of posts that began 70 metres south on the Rue Delvas, paralleled the Rue Deleval for 180 metres, then curved towards the German breastwork. A shallow wall of sandbags across the road connected to 54 Battalion, whose posts were in a ditch that ran eastwards towards the farm track opposite the *Pension pour les Chiens*, the dog kennels in the two buildings to the left of the Kennedy Crucifix. The section held by Captain Gibbins bent back to the breastwork short of the track, on the far side of which were Lieutenant Colonel Toll and some of 31 Battalion. Lieutenant Colonel Cass set up 54 Battalion's headquarters in a luxurious *Wohngraben* 45 metres past the eastern end of the park, where Brompton Road struck the German line after being extended across No Man's Land during the battle. It started at the farm buildings on the Rue Petillon.

No sooner had 14 Brigade arrived than Second Lieutenant Bachschneider led 10 Company 3/16 BRIR and the remnants of 12 Company 3/21 BRIR against 53 Battalion's flank in the field to the west. The few men from A Company in the breastwork pulled out, sparking a retirement by those around them. Shortly afterwards, Arblaster was shocked to see the Germans heading along the vacant

RUE PETILLON — AUSTRALIAN LINE — 14 BRIGADE

ADVANCED LINE 14 BRIGADE

The area occupied by 14 Brigade and the gap between it and the right of 8 Brigade's screen as seen from the Australian Memorial Park.

line behind him towards the Rue Delvas. With anyone who could be spared, he held them for an hour until a lack of grenades forced him back to the advanced line. By then the Germans were virtually at the entrance to the park and only barricades hastily thrown up on the orders of Lieutenant Colonel McConaghy, commanding from 55 Battalion's headquarters fifty metres from the road, stopped them going further. Sergeant Law left the advanced line to bayonet a machine gun crew firing from the area of the crucifix.

Advancing from the direction of Delaporte Farm shortly after 1 am, companies from 1 and 2/16 BRIR renewed the attack along the breastwork and simultaneously struck 53 Battalion's right flank in the occupied ditches. At Arblaster's urging, Captain Murray, whose post was near the sandbag wall across the Rue Delvas, sent a stream of men to keep them at bay. But the Germans were too strong. Some crossed the road at the breastwork, while others worked their way behind the ditches to fire into the rear of 53 Battalion's advanced line. As a last resort Arblaster led a charge against them but it was instantly mown down.

With the pocket west of the Rue Delvas driven in, the Germans were now able to surge up the road and into an empty ditch along the tramway. They shot into the back of the advanced line on the eastern side until Lieutenant Agassiz silenced them by firing a shoulder mounted Lewis Gun from it towards the park. Meanwhile, Sergeant Stringer threw grenades from the parapet of the breastwork on the

CELLAR FARM

FROMELLES   KENNEDY CRUCIFIX

northern side of the park entrance to stop the Germans there. Then Lieutenant Denoon and fifty men, moving along both parapet and parados, regained seventy metres of the breastwork, of which the Germans took back half. Lasting an hour, this herculean bomb fight kept them on the road.

Crossing the Rue Delvas east of the crucifix at 2.30 am, 1/21 BRIR and part of 1/20 BRIR assaulted astride the farm track. Lieutenant Colonel Toll and Captain Gibbins held the attack but further east the Germans reached their vacant front line and rolled along it to the Kastenweg, forcing the remnants of 8 Brigade to charge through them to the Australian line. Toll's men left after being cut off from Gibbins, who led several counterattacks along the parapet as the Germans reoccupied this part of their breastwork.

By now, the rest of 1/16 BRIR had poured across the Teufelsgraben, a strongpoint between Rouge Bancs and Delaporte Farm, and the entire perimeter was being pressed. The attack penetrated the advanced line between the park and the farm track and the Australians, ordered to withdraw, had to mount yet another rearwards charge to the breastwork, which Gibbins' rearguard was holding at the head of the Brompton Road extension. Safety lay at the other end of it.

In the May 1915 battle, 24 and 25 Brigades from the 8th Division assaulted astride the Rue Delvas. On the western side, most of 2/Northants were mowed down by enfilade fire from the Sugarloaf and 2/E. Lancs suffered the same fate between them and the road. On the eastern side, 25 Brigade enjoyed more success, with 2/Rifle Brigade and 1/Royal Irish Rifles sweeping over the breastwork between the park and the tree line to Rouge Bancs, the Kennedy Crucifix marking the limit of their advance. From Cordonnerie Farm on the far side of the tree line, the Kensingtons captured Delangré Farm after two mines were blown under the breastwork at the right of the prominent copse. As with the Australians later on, the wide gaps between the penetrations assisted the German counterattacks, and the British were forced out with dreadful casualties.

The unfinished mine gallery below Nephew Trench as it was in 1997.
(M. Delebarre)

The blockhouses in the Australian Memorial Park at war's end. (M. Delebarre)

Turning to the blockhouses in the park, the ASBF says they were built in 1917 and their damaged state reflects the postwar efforts of farmers to remove them rather than the wear and tear of battle. Exploration by the ASBF has revealed that the blockhouse closest to the road was an infantry shelter and the one furthest from it a stores dump. The centre blockhouse was a miners' shelter covering the shaft head of an unfinished mine gallery below Nephew Trench, the name the British gave to the German line here. Partially collapsed now, it juts 38 metres towards their line.

A Car Tour of the Battlefield and Related Areas

This tour covers the attacks of both divisions, parts of the German line, the British and German rear areas and the cemeteries. It starts in Sailly (1), where Haking and McCay had their headquarters and part of 15 Brigade was billeted. Head west on the D945 and Anzac Cemetery (2) is on the right after 800 metres. Captain Norman Gibbins at I.A.5 is the best known of the Fromelles fallen buried there. Nineteen more Australians rest in the Canadian cemetery across the road. After another 1.5 kilometres, turn left onto the D18 for Laventie. On arriving at the northern edge of the town, turn left again onto the D166, where

The 61st Division Memorial in Laventie.

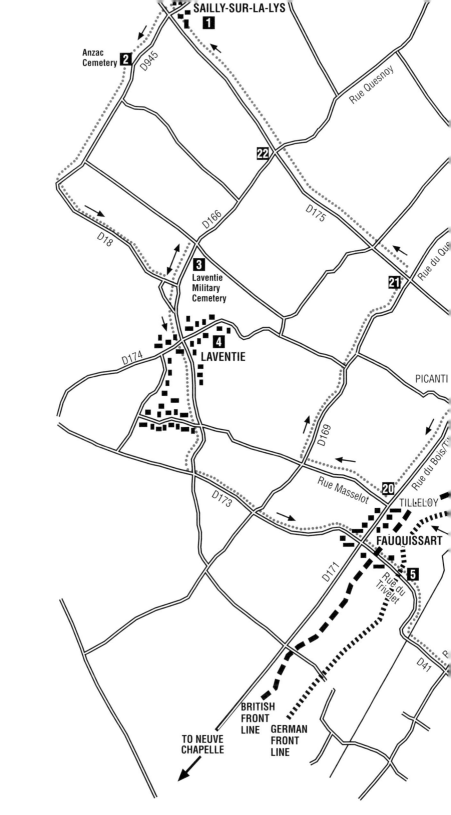

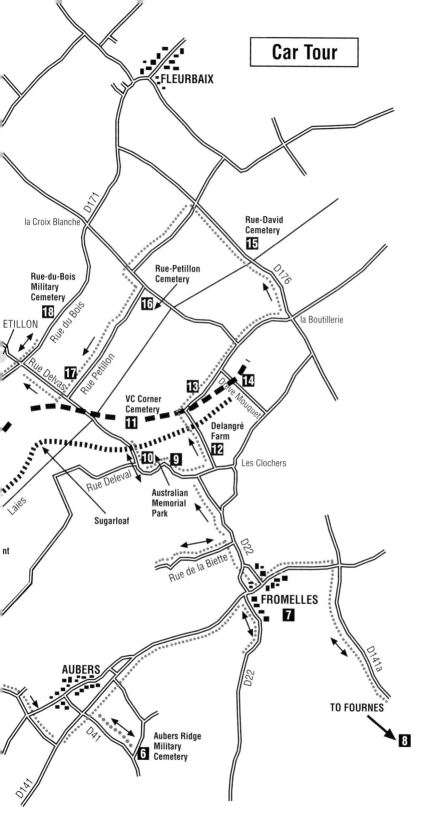

Car Tour

Laventie Military Cemetery **(3)** is signposted after 500 metres. It contains many dead from 184 Brigade, most notably Lieutenant Colonel Beer and Captain Church at II.E.17 and II.E.23 respectively. The 61st Division's headquarters at L.35.b.8.9 was also in this area.

As you join the main road through Laventie **(4)**, 183 Brigade's headquarters was on the right of the intersection. Many of the 61st Division's units were billeted in or near the town and some of its third and fourth battalions stood by there during the attack. A divisional memorial is on the northern facade of the Town Hall, which is next to the church on the crossroads at the town centre. Bearing the 61st's crest and badges of the constituent regiments, it was unveiled on 22 April 1935. Cockshy House, 182 Brigade's headquarters, was 680 metres down the D174 opposite.

Continue southwards through Laventie and follow the D173 as it curves southeast to cross the Rue du Bois in Fauquissart, after which it becomes the Rue du Trivelet. This road was the western boundary of the Fromelles attack and the 61st Division's right flank. Its line straddled the Rue du Trivelet 160 metres from the crossroads. Held by 3/17 BRIR, the German line went over 300 metres further south **(5)**. On reaching it, part of 2/7 Warwicks faced west to cover Captain Donaldson's men as they dashed to the support line 100 metres beyond.

At the sharp bend in the Rue du Trivelet, look left to see the Laies knifing through the fields towards VC Corner Cemetery, and then right, towards Neuve Chapelle two kilometres upstream. The first British offensive of the war, in March 1915, and the main attack on Aubers Ridge on 9 May 1915, started either side of this village. After crossing the Laies at an abrupt left turn, the road heads to Aubers, whose church spire breaks the ridgeline, as the D41 or Rue d'Enfer. Blockhouses line the Rue Neuve, the farm road that enters on the left at the roundabout after 600 metres. Turn left onto the D141 after another 1.3 kilometres, and then right at the resumption of the D41, which is signposted for Herlies. Aubers Ridge Military Cemetery **(6)** is 750 metres down the road. Resting at VI.B.9, Captain William Simms of 2/6 Warwicks is among the many British and Australian dead who lie there.

Return to the D141 and turn right for Fromelles. The German line on the ridge ran to the left of the road, although a concrete observation post appears on the right after a half kilometre. Its elevation overcame the flatness of the crest which, together with the trees and crops, precludes good views from the road today of the low ground to the north over which the front lines ran. As Hitler reputedly visited the blockhouse on the left, built by Bau-Pionier-Kompanie 4 500 metres from Fromelles, during his 1940 battlefield tour, he was said to have

The Fromelles Museum. The ladder was recovered from a mine gallery in the Tadpole in 1994.

sheltered in it during the battle. But recently unearthed photographs show him minutely examining the N.16.c.1.1 blockhouse, which was in a less obvious location below the ridge. It seems a likelier Führerbunker!

As the D22 looms on the western edge of Fromelles, 'Bayern Nord', 16 BRIR's battle headquarters at N.23.c.0.3, is in the trees off to the right. It is on private land but can be viewed by taking the D22 for 700 metres, at which point it turns sharply south, and looking back across the fields. Returning to the D141, enter Fromelles **(7)** and visit the museum on the second floor of the town hall and school building, which is on the left 150 metres past the junction with the D22. It contains many relics collected by the ASBF as well as the marble

IN DIESEM QUAR- -TIER LAG 1916
UNSER FUEHRER
ADOLF HITLER
ALS SOLDAT
DES BAYR. JNF. RGT. LIST
TECHN. ABT. IX   20. 4. 1942

The marble plaque fixed to the wall of Hitler's wartime billet in Fournes.

plaque the Germans put up in April 1942 on Hitler's 1916 billet in Fournes.

If you want to visit Fournes **(8)**, continue on the D141 for another kilometre and take the D141a on the right. Brigadier General Kiefhaber commanded 16 BRIR from the town during the May 1915

966 Rue Faidherbe, Fournes-en-Weppes, Hitler's address in 1916.

battle and the 6th BR Division's reserve battalions were regularly stationed there. 1/20 BRIR deployed from it against the Australians only to be clobbered by artillery on reaching Fromelles. Hitler's billet, the old butchery at 966 Rue Faidherbe, is next to a pharmacy. The supporting pins for the plaque still protrude from the front wall. Fournes German Cemetery is behind the hedge at the rear of the yard of Les Haute de France warehouse in Rue Raoult.

Return to Fromelles, head right on the D22 and stop at the church. The Germans built a concrete observation post inside the original church. Some stained glass and a table from it, and the first Kennedy Crucifix, are in the new one. Despite the trees and the urban sprawl, a brief walk around this area conveys some idea of the views it commanded over the plain. As you drive down the road, the gentle slope of the ridge becomes apparent. To see the 'new' Hitler blockhouse at N.16.c.1.1, turn left onto the Rue de la Biette after 350 metres and stop 800 metres along where, on the right of a kink in the road, raised banks enclose a rough paddock containing two ponds. The blockhouse is beyond the far end. The Australian Memorial Park is a kilometre north. Some men from 14 Brigade almost came this far in their search for the second and third German lines. Be aware that crop growth can hide the blockhouse.

Going back to the D22, turn left and take the left branch of the fork at the bottom of the hill. A memorial to Sergeant K.W. Bramble of 609 Squadron, whose Spitfire was downed here on 21 July 1941, stands at another fork 500 metres further on. Head left again and, after about 150 metres, the elevated bank of a small pond almost touches the road. Walking through his own barrage, Lieutenant Colonel Toll reached this point in his quest for a clearly defined German support line. The Grashof strongpoint, which he could see, was in the field 270 metres south.

After bending to the right, the road makes a ninety-degree turn leftwards at the dog kennels, opposite which a farm track goes north into the fields **(9)**. The ditch occupied by 54 Battalion ran from the direction of the old corner café to the west but swung back short of the track to the German breastwork, which straddled the track 210 metres rearwards near the bush-covered blockhouses. Some 160 metres east of the track, 31 Battalion's advanced company manned a derelict trench that went through the thick tree line to the right of the telegraph poles. As the yawing gap between the two battalions was never bridged, 1/20 and 1/21 BRIR's counterattack along the track soon split them. Passing the Kennedy Crucifix, study the battle from the Australian Memorial Park **(10)** and then visit VC Corner Cemetery **(11)**. Parking is not easy there so you might consider walking. It is only 200 metres away.

Retrace your route to the Bramble memorial and turn left to reach the Rue de la Cordonnerie after 200 metres. The Türkenecke strongpoint at N.16.b.2.7 was south of the corner, an area dotted by blockhouses, and the Hofgarten machine gun, which troubled 31 Battalion, fired from Les Clochers, the hamlet at the end of the road 220 metres east. Reserves from 20 and 21 BRIR in both locations reinforced Delangré Farm **(12)**, which stood on the patch of torn ground on the right of the Rue de la Cordonnerie 200 metres along. Briefly held by the Kensingtons in May 1915, it vexed the Australians in July 1916. The gated grass path at the start of the wooded area leads to the *minenwerfer* position excavated by the ASBF. After jumping the road here, the Kastenweg ran on its left to the front line 250 metres north. Krinks XI was in shellholes on its right just beyond the farm.

The German breastwork followed the path along the fence beside the large shed, which is at the back of the house sheltered by the prominent copse that you saw from the Australian Memorial Park. You can track it to the park by looking along the line of telegraph poles through the clearing on the left. In the opposite direction, it slanted northeastwards past the three blockhouses in the field. Mouquet Farm, which tormented 32 Battalion, is on their right half a kilometre away. The British line crossed the road near the white tank at the front of the house. No Man's Land was about 100 metres wide at this point. The

AUSTRALIAN MINE CRATER

CORDONNERIE FARM

No Man's Land where the Australian mine was blown.

Australian mine exploded in it to the right of the road, the earlier British ones under the German line to the left, which was the area from which 1/21 BRIR raided 58 Battalion on 15 July 1916.

Captain Allen's switch trench, which almost crossed No Man's Land, started in front of Cordonnerie Farm (13), whose buildings back onto a black shed in front of Cellar Farm and are on the left after the road swings sharply right. Depending on whether the field at the end of it is in crop or not, the farm track that heads west from the bend ends in the Australian front line near the boundary between 8 and 14 Brigades. As the road heads northeast, the British line was on the right and held by 60 Brigade. Pause after 500 metres at the Drève Mouquet (14), on which the Tadpole stood 300 metres from the junction. In 1994 the ASBF unearthed a 30-metre long mine gallery running from it. Mouquet Farm is 150 metres further south. Neither 60 Brigade nor the artillery could prevent the machine guns in both strongpoints pouring fire into the Australian flank.

Continue to the Boutillerie crossroads, keeping an eye out for the ruins of l'Abbaye Chartreaux on the right. Turn left onto the D176, the Rue des Davids, where many Fromelles dead rest in Rue-David Cemetery (15) 900 metres along. Head left again at the next crossroads and at the T-junction, and then right onto the Rue Petillon after 150 metres. Rue-Petillon Military Cemetery (16) is next to the site of Eaton Hall dressing station. Chaplain Maxted of 54 Battalion and Major Harrison, its second-in-command, rest at I.K.2 and I.D.20 respectively. Cellar Farm Avenue began 230 metres past the cemetery and ran to the farm of the same name 650 metres southeast. Brompton Road parallelled it 350 metres further on.

Le Trou Aid Post Cemetery (17), where Brigadier General Lowry Cole lies at E22, appears after another 250 metres. Brigadier General Elliott's headquarters and the aid post were in Le Trou hamlet opposite, which Pinney's Avenue linked to the front line 500 metres south. To reach the front line in 15 Brigade's sector, walk 200 metres down the farm track that runs southwest from the junction with the Rue Delvas. From this location, 15 Machine Gun Company engaged the Sugarloaf, whose apex was 370 metres south. Delaporte Farm, Fromelles and the Australian Memorial Park are to its left.

Now head north on the Rue Delvas to the Petillon crossroads and turn right onto the Rue du Bois, which VC Avenue crossed 130 metres along. Dugout corrugated iron is stacked against the black tin barn and screw pickets have been put to good use amongst the soft fruit bushes near the spot. Rue-du-Bois Military Cemetery (18) is 250 metres further on the left. Many 2/1 Bucks and 15 Brigade dead rest there, including Major McCrae, the commander of 60 Battalion, at I.F.33. Passing through Croix Blanche crossroads, where 30 Battalion held its post-battle roll call, the Rue du Bois ends in Fleurbaix, which was an Australian billeting centre. On leaving the cemetery, though, you should head back to Petillon, from where it ran behind the British line.

Bond Street, the inter-divisional boundary, ran southeast near house number 152, 350 metres past the crossroads. Picantin **(19)** was directly behind the centre of 184 Brigade's line. Sutherland Avenue, its boundary with 183 Brigade, began 300 metres further along the D171, now the Rue de Tilleloy, from the clearing on the left. The irrigation ditch behind number 52 in Tilleloy crossed 182 Brigade's line after 200 metres and the apex of the Wick Salient after another 200 metres.

Many soldiers from the 61st Division were tired out before the attack from carrying gas cylinders back to a dump on the Rue Masselot **(20)**, the next road on the right. Apple House, 2/6 Warwick's headquarters, was on the left 350 metres along, and both Warwicks assault battalions deployed their reserve companies nearby. Ironically, a German cemetery occupies the area now. Masselot Post, from which a communication trench ran parallel to the road, was also on the left half a kilometre north. Now turn right onto the D169 and, on passing 13th London Graveyard, look north, where 184 Brigade's headquarters

The D169 (Rue du Quesnes) meets the D175.

stood on the parallel road, the Rue Verte, at M.6.a.5.8. The British artillery and, closer to the D175, the Australian artillery, fired from the fields around you.

Head left on reaching the D175 **(21)**, which took the Australians to the battle. The D169 beyond it is the Rue du Quesnes, where their third battalions assembled. Their fourth battalions waited on the Rue Quesnoy (now Bataille), which crosses the D175 two kilometres north **(22)**. Continue into Sailly. Its German cemetery, which contains 5,400 graves, is 800 metres east on the D945.

Walk One: The Australian Attack

This eight-kilometre (5 miles) walk covers the 5th Division's attack. Start by studying the battle from the Australian Memorial Park **(1)** and then try to visualise the night of 19 July 1916. Arcing flares and the flashes of exploding grenades, whose dull crumps often drown out the harsh cacophony of machine gun and rifle fire, light up the area. An acrid smoke cloud makes breathing difficult. Mud covered figures splash along the ditches to the road in response to the unceasing call for more grenades and men to throw them. The desperation in the voices leaves no doubt that things are critical there. Awful moans come from the wounded sheltering in the German breastwork, which rises like a dam wall against the night sky. You wonder how anyone could survive. Most did not.

Head south on the Rue Delvas and turn right onto the Rue Deleval **(2)**. The Heckengraben, along which companies from 1 and 2/16 BRIR moved to counterattack 14 Brigade's right flank, ran from the rear to Delaporte Farm, which is on the left after 300 metres. As the road swings to the right at the Orchard House and just before the small chapel, a farm track goes into the field. Depending on whether the crops are in, it ends on the German front line between the Sugarloaf and the Australian Memorial Park near the boundary between 14 and 15 Brigades. The dead and wounded of 60 Battalion and of 59 Battalion next to them covered the ground on the left, back to and beyond the Laies, whose line is ahead of you.

Return to the Rue Delvas and continue past the Kennedy Crucifix. Some men from 14 Brigade crossed here and kept going in their search for the German support line. The road makes a right-angle turn at the *Pension pour les Chiens*, opposite which a farm track goes north **(3)**. Walk 50 metres along it and look northeastwards. Sections of derelict trench running in that direction were occupied by 8 Brigade, whose right flank, held by B Company 31 Battalion, was 160 metres away.

141

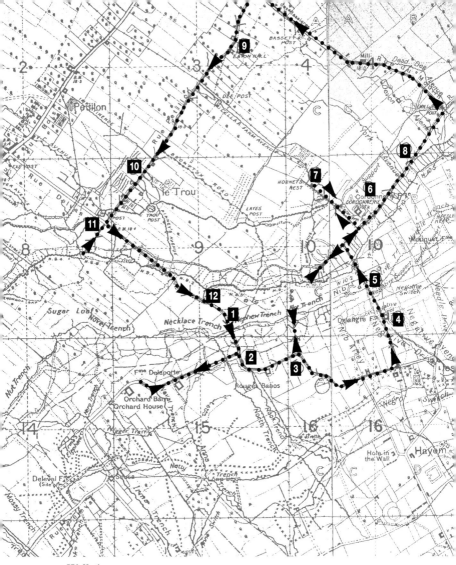

Walk 1.

Manned by 32 Battalion, the rest of the line went through the copse to the Kastenweg. Walk another 70 metres and look west towards the old corner café. You are now level with 54 Battalion's ditch, which did not meet the track but swung back to the breastwork, 90 metres further along and in the vicinity of the bush-covered blockhouses on the right.

Noting that the telegraph poles approximate the breastwork's easterly line, face south towards Fromelles on reaching it. Lieutenant Colonel Toll and the rest of 31 Battalion were on your left and Captain

Gibbins's men on your right but the 270-metre gap between the inner flanks of 8 and 14 Brigades to your front remained open. Having come down the road from Fromelles, 1/20 and 1/21 BRIR attacked astride the track at 2.30 am and overran 31 Battalion's advanced line. Reaching the breastwork on Toll's left, they barrelled along it to the Kastenweg, forcing 8 Brigade's chaotic withdrawal. Toll's group pulled out after being cut off from Gibbins and 14 Brigade withdrew a few hours later.

Before leaving, think of men up to their knees in water struggling to make a parapet from mud-filled sandbags, of wounded drowning, of isolated groups fighting on until a grenade finished them off. Think too, of 25 Brigade crossing this field in the 8th Division's attack a year earlier, and of Brigadier Lowry Cole, who fell while urging them on.

Just past the next bend in the road, the raised bank of a pond on the right at N.16.a.4.5 marks the end of Lieutenant Colonel Toll's attempt to find the German support trench. He walked through the Australian barrage to it. Continue to the memorial to Sergeant K.W. Bramble of 609 Squadron, whose Spitfire crashed here on 21 July 1941, and head left at the fork to the Rue de la Cordonnerie, 200 metres distant. The Türkenecke strongpoint lay to the south at N.16.b.2.7, an area where blockhouses can be seen. Les Clochers, the hamlet 220 metres eastward at the end the road, was the site of the Hofgarten machine gun, which forced 31 Battalion to ground. 20 and 21 BRIR's reserves in both locations reinforced the remnants of 10 Company 3/21 BRIR at Delangré Farm **(4)**, which was in the copse on the right of the Rue de la Cordonnerie.

A gated grass path at the near edge of the copse leads to the *minenwerfer* pit at N.10.d.2.1 that the ASBF excavated in 1995. The farm strongpoint stood on the mutilated ground further on. It neutralised the blocks in the Kastenweg, which crossed the road next to the gate and ran along the left side. Krinks XI set up their two Lewis guns in shellholes near the crumbling shed at the northern edge of the farm site, from where the Germans on the higher ground of the strongpoint were silhouetted against the night sky. Together with 32 Battalion's flanking posts under Lieutenant Mills, which were on the far side of the Kastenweg, they blocked 2/21 BRIR's counterattack along the communication trench.

The German breastwork **(5)** ran along the fence that extends from the right of the road past the large shed at the back of the distinctive copse that you saw from the Australian Memorial Park. You can see the park from the copse by looking west along the telegraph poles, which

The view southwest from the German breastwork in the area held by Lieutenant Colonel Toll and 31 Battalion.

generally follow the line of the breastwork. In the other direction, it passed the three blockhouses in the field, which were probably infantry shelters. The buildings around the prominent barn to their right 500 metres away are slightly south of the Mouquet Farm strongpoint site. Its enfilade advantage against the Australians' left flank is obvious. Their line straddled the road near the white tank on the far side of the copse. Their mine went off in No Man's Land to the right of the road, the two British ones under the German line to the left. 1/21 BRIR raided 58 Battalion from it on 15 July 1916.

Now walk to the sharp bend, from which the buildings of Cordonnerie Farm **(6)** are 100 metres distant at N.10.a.8.4. Take the farm track on the left and, after 230 metres, you will be on the Australian front line 40 metres short of the boundary between 8 and 14 Brigades. The narrowness of No Man's Land, which greatly helped their attack, is evident from the park and the telegraph poles denoting the German line opposite. But it also accounted for the pummeling the

Looking west along the German front line from Delangré Farm towards the Australian Memorial Park.

KENNEDY
CRUCIFIX

ADVANCED LINE
14 BRIGADE

DELAPORTE
FARM

AUSTRALIAN MEMORIAL
PARK

Australians took from their own artillery, especially in 31 Battalion, before they went over here. The rumpled mounds on the left as you return to the road enclose the moat of a medieval farm. Mine Avenue ran along the near side. *Minenwerfers*, no doubt including the one behind Delangré Farm, blew in its junction with the front line a few metres away on the right, obstructing 30 Battalion's move forward.

At Cordonnerie Farm, turn left onto the farm track beside it for Cellar Farm **(7)** at the end. The mines supporting the Kensingtons' attack in May 1915 were blown from the 300 Yard Line, which ran between the two farms. In the field on the right, the ASBF is excavating some deep dugouts that were begun in September 1916 to accommodate a battalion. The pump piping and its wooden sheaths are in perfect condition and thousands of rat pawprints pattern the concrete lining the four shaftheads. Cellar Farm Avenue passed through Cellar Farm on its northward track to the Rue Petillon, which it met to the left of Rue-Petillon Military Cemetery. Its Cross of Sacrifice is clearly

Cellar Farm Avenue.

BROMPTON ROAD

CELLAR FARM AVENUE

RUE-PETILLON MILITARY
CEMETERY

ASBF excavation of underground accommodation for British troops at Cellar Farm.

visible. The farm was also the starting point of Mine Avenue. German shelling smashed both communication trenches and the line between them before 1/21 BRIR's raid on 58 Battalion.

Return to the road and turn left past Cordonnerie Farm. The switch trench Captain Allen's men dug left the line in front of the farm and would have met the German line close to the shed at the back of the copse had it been completed. As you walk the 400 metres to the Drève Mouquet **(8)**, the British line was held by 60 Brigade and ran to your right. The German line crossed the Drève Mouquet 300 metres south, at which point the Tadpole stood on a slight rise on the left of the road. A ladder that the ASBF recovered from a 30-metre mine gallery they found running from it in 1994 is displayed in the Fromelles museum. Mouquet Farm is 150 metres south of the Tadpole. Untroubled by the Australian artillery and suppressive fire from 60 Brigade, both strongpoints and the line to their west caused no end of trouble for the left flank of the attack and the men digging the switch trench.

After another 300 metres, turn left onto the D175 and again onto the Rue Petillon 1.1 kilometres later. Resting at I.K.2 and I.D.20 respectively, Chaplain Maxted of 54 Battalion and Major Harrison, its second-in-command, whose remains were found and identified from his cigarette case in 1927, are among the Fromelles dead who lie in Rue-Petillon Military Cemetery **(9)**. It is next to the site of Eaton Hall dressing station. Cellar Farm Avenue began 230 metres beyond and stretched 650 metres southeastward to the farm, from which you looked back to this location earlier. Starting 350 metres further on, Brompton Road parallelled it. Brigadier General Lowry Cole sleeps at E22 in beautiful Le Trou Aid Post Cemetery **(10)**, which is on the right after another 250 metres.

Brigadier General Elliott's headquarters and the aid post were in the hamlet on the other side of the road, from which Pinney's Avenue ran to the front line 500 metres south. Now look southeast from the corner of the Rue Petillon and the Rue Delvas towards Cellar Farm and the black shed behind Cordonnerie Farm. Heavily shelled in the hours before the attack, the Australian line stretched from there to the nearer side of the farm buildings directly in front of you, on the other side of which is VC Corner Cemetery, before crossing the Rue Delvas. Walk 200 metres down the farm track **(11)** that runs southwest from the corner to reach the location from which 15 Machine Gun Company fired on the Sugarloaf. The track peters out just short of where Rhondda Sap crossed the interdivisonal boundary.

If the field has just been harvested, you can reach the Sugarloaf from the 200-metre point on the track by heading south for 370 metres. As you walk, imagine being under torrential fire from several machine guns every step of the way. Spent cartridge cases, which still come to the surface, litter the site of the apex and are a sign that you have arrived at the right place. Striking the Laies means you have veered to the left. The German line ran to the Australian Memorial Park, and the first house on the Rue Deleval to the south is Delaporte Farm. For 3/16 BRIR's perspective, look back to your starting point. As you return, consider the folly of putting the interdivisional boundary so close to the Sugarloaf that when 184 Brigade was decimated in front of it, 3/16 BRIR had 15 Brigade in enfilade to your right. Think, too, of 58 Battalion's suicidal attack.

VC Avenue crossed the Rue Delvas 60 metres past the track junction and the Australian line went over after another 300 metres. The road bridges the Laies, along which a German machine gun fired, and passes VC Corner Cemetery (12). Both are in the old No Man's Land. On your way back to the park, pause at the cemetery to consider the aftermath of the battle. The fields around it were carpeted with dead and wounded, whom their cobbers tried to bring back in nightly forays. Wracked by pain, driven mad by thirst and the attentions of ants and flies, many could not be recovered and met an agonising end. Some of them lie in these hallowed grounds. All of them are named on the wall at the far end.

Walk Two: The British Attack

The 61st Division's line ran south of the D171 (Rue du Bois/Tilleloy). Though gaps between the houses offer good views over the fields it crossed in each brigade sector, access tracks are few. Hence the following walk parallels the opposing front lines. It is about nine kilometres (5.6 miles) long.

Start on the Rue du Bois at the Petillon crossroads (1). Bond Street,

Bond Street, the interdivisional boundary.

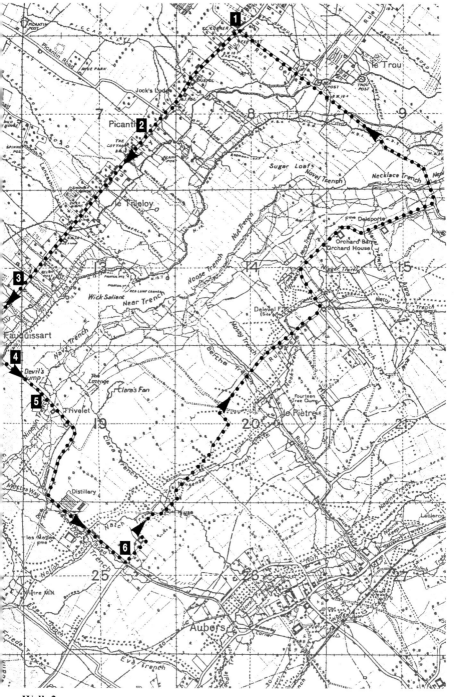

Walk 2.

2/6 WARWICKS

Looking south towards the Wick Salient from 2/6 Warwicks' front line.

the inter-divisional boundary, headed southeast 350 metres away. The track to the left of house number 152, which has a sign reading *Oeufs et Poulets de Grains* at the front and a big shed at the back, goes close and gets you to the 300-Yard Line. Continue to Picantin **(2)**, where the headquarters of 2/1 Bucks and 2/4 Berks were co-located 500 metres north at Hyde Park on the Rue de Lille and an RAP stood on the corner. The track opposite ends at the 300 Yard Line near the boundary between the two assault battalions. Wayward Australian shelling blew up a gas cylinder in 2/1 Bucks' line on the left of it the night before the attack. Sutherland Avenue, the boundary between 183 and 184 Brigades, started from the clearing near the Fauquissart road sign 300 metres along.

Both front lines can be reached by following the track alongside the irrigation ditch that cuts southeastwards through the field behind house number 52 in Tilleloy. Running parallel to the road, the British breastwork crossed the ditch 200 metres in, and the apex of the Wick Salient, against which 2/6 Warwicks were shattered, was 200 metres from it. British artillery observers directed fire from houses scattered along the length of the Rue Tilleloy that you have just walked.

The next road on the right, the Rue Masselot **(3)**, was a main artery to the 61st Division's line. Many of its soldiers were exhausted before the attack by having to lug gas cylinders along this road to the dump from which they had carried them to the line five weeks earlier. Both Warwicks assault battalions held their reserve companies near 2/6 Warwicks' headquarters at the Apple House, 350 metres north. A German cemetery occupies the area now. Masselot Street communication trench ran to the west of its namesake and crossed the D171 180 metres from it.

At Fauquissart, turn left onto the D173, the Rue du Trivelet, which was the attack's western limit and the 61st Division's right flank. The British front line (4) crossed it after 160 metres. Stokes mortars were emplaced on the right of the road there and 200 metres southwest to support 2/7 Warwicks. Before the German breastwork (5), held by 3/17 BRIR, went over 300 metres further on, it ran along the left of the road for 100 metres. Part of 2/7 Warwicks occupied this section to form a block facing west. But neither they nor the Stokes mortars could stop the machine guns on that side of the road flaying the men Captain Donaldson led to the support line, which they nonetheless reached at a point in the field 100 metres northeast. Their short-lived success was the high water mark of the British attack.

With binoculars, VC Corner Cemetery is visible to the east. Look left as the Rue du Trivelet heads sharply right to see the Laies slicing through the fields towards it. The first British offensive of the war, in March 1915, and the main attack on Aubers Ridge on 9 May 1915, began either side of Neuve Chapelle, two kilometres upstream in the opposite direction. To the south, the spire of Aubers church rises above the ridge.

The next perpendicular bend spans the Laies. At the roundabout 650 metres past it, turn left onto the Rue Neuve, a minor road (6). Eventually becoming the Rue Deleval, it was dotted with strongpoints and shelters that gave depth to the front line. Many of the blockhouses, though, date from 1917. They include the one on the left 700 meters in and the huge command bunker, Dachau, built by 81 Regiment Pionier-Kompanie, a kilometre further near the site of Deleval Farm.

Continue to the Orchard House, now *La Ferme Equestre L'Hippocrate*, opposite which is a small chapel. The Sugarloaf was 450

17 BRIR's front line on the Rue du Trivelet, which was captured by 2/7 Warwicks.

metres north of it. To get some idea of 3/16 BRIR's view of 184 Brigade's attack, look northwest. Note the flatness of the ground, which offered no cover, and remember the width of No Man's Land, 370 metres. The feat of Captain Church and his men in getting as far as the strongpoint was as miraculous as their fate was inevitable. Return to the Rue Deleval and, after passing Delaporte Farm on the right, head left on the Rue Delvas. You might care to pause at the Australian Memorial Park and VC Corner Cemetery on your way back to the Petillon crossroads.

Walk Three: The Ridge

Though it was well behind the 6th BR Division's front line, Aubers Ridge gave the Germans good observation over the battlefield. It was also the objective of the attack in May 1915 and prominent in General Haking's thinking fourteen months later. This walk includes the ridge and is 5.5 kilometres (3.5 miles) long.

Start at Fromelles church **(1)**. It contains the first Kennedy Crucifix, and some stained glass and a table from the original church. Trees and houses have sprung up on the slope but you can still

Walk 3.

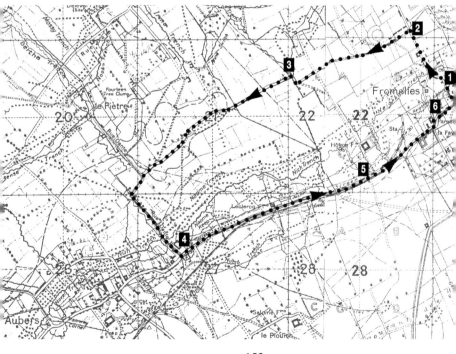

appreciate the views the Germans had over the plain from here. Though the original church was destroyed, the concrete observation post they built inside it remained unscathed.

Head 350 metres down the road and turn left at the Rue de la Biette **(2)**. Shortly after passing the sports ground prominently marked 'Fromelles FC' about 650 metres in, it kinks noticeably right then left **(3)**. Walk northwards until the bushy bank around the rough

The original Fromelles church. (M. Delebarre)

paddock on the right peters out and the blockhouse that recently rediscovered photographs show Hitler examining closely while touring his old battlefields in June 1940 is in front of you at N.16.c.1.1. According to the ASBF, Bau-Pionier-Kompanie 13 built it in 1915. The Australian Memorial Park is a kilometre north. Searching for the second and third German lines, some men from 14 Brigade nearly came this far. If the crops are high, the blockhouse and the view north may be hidden.

Two kilometres and several blockhouses later, the Rue de la Biette swings hard left and starts an imperceptible climb towards Aubers. Some houses on this stretch have blockhouses in their grounds. Turn left on reaching the T-junction and follow the road around to the D141 on the crest **(4)**, where you will see a concrete observation post off to the right. It was originally built inside a cottage for concealment. As the flatness of the crest masks the plain below, the Germans sited their line on the ridge up to 200 metres to the left of the D141, where the ground starts to fall away. To reach it, take any of the tracks that run north as the road heads to Fromelles.

For many years, the infantry shelter **(5)** built by Bau-Pionier-Kompanie 4 on the left half a kilometre short of the village was called the Hitler blockhouse because Hitler supposedly sheltered in it during the battle and stopped there on his 1940 tour. He may well have done. But the photographs of Hitler at the N.16.c.1.1, a fighting blockhouse below the ridge and closer to the action, make it a better bet. 'Bayern Nord', 16 BRIR's battle headquarters at N.23.c.0.3, is in the trees on the right of the D22 at the western edge of Fromelles.

The excellent museum on the second floor of the town hall and

The 'old' Hitler bunker (below), and the 'new' (above).

school building **(6)** 150 metres past the junction displays a wealth of artefacts that the ASBF has recovered from the battlefield, some extremely moving, and the marble plaque the Germans fixed to the wall of Hitler's 1916 billet in Fournes in April 1942. It was damaged when thrown down after the village's liberation in 1944. Head left at the village centre to return to the church.

SELECT BIBLIOGRAPHY

I relied heavily in the writing of this guide on instructions, orders and reports relating to the Fromelles attack and the war diaries of the divisions, brigades and battalions that fought in it, all of which the Australian War Memorial in Canberra and the Public Record Office in London hold between them. The files I found most useful, as well as personal manuscripts, are listed in the notes at the end of each chapter.

The following secondary sources describe the battle, as well as relevant aspects of the attack on Aubers Ridge:

1. R. Austin, *Black and Gold. The History of the 29th Battalion AIF 1915-18* (Slouch Hat Publications, 1997)
2. C.E.W. Bean, *Anzac to Amiens* (AWM, 1968)
3. C.E.W. Bean, *The Official History of Australia in the War of 1914-1918. III. The AIF in France: 1916* (Angus & Robertson, 1942)
4. A. Bristow, *A Serious Disappointment* (Pen and Sword, 1995)
5. M. Brown, *The Imperial War Museum Book of the Western Front* (Motorbooks, 1994)
6. P. Charlton, *Pozières* (Methuen, 1986)
7. H.T. Chidgey, *Black Square Memories* (Blackwell, 1924)
8. R.S. Corfield, *Don't Forget Me, Cobber* (Corfield & Co., 2000)
9. R.S. Corfield, *Hold Hard, Cobbers, I* (57/60 Bn Association, 1992)
10. W.H. Downing, *To The Last Ridge* (Duffy & Snellgrove, 1998)
11. J.E. Edmonds, *Military Operations: France and Belgium, 1915. II. Battles of Aubers Ridge, Festubert and Loos* (Macmillan, 1928)
12. A.D. Ellis, *The Story of the Fifth Australian Division* (Hodder and Stoughton, 1920)
13. A.H. Farrar-Hockley, *Somme* (Pan, 1983)
14. R. Graves, *Goodbye To All That* (Penguin, 1976)
15. R.C.B. Haking, *Company Training* (Hugh Rees, 1913)
16. R.H. Knyvett, *Over There with the Australians* (Hodder and Stoughton, 1918)
17. B.H. Liddell Hart, *History of the First World War* (Cassell, 1970)
18. R.E. Lording (aka 'A. Tiveychoc'), *There and Back* (RSL of Australia, 1935)
19. L. MacDonald, *1915* (Headline, 1993)
20. L. Macdonald, *Somme* (Michael Joseph, 1983)
21. R. McMullin, *Pompey Elliott* (Scribe, 2002)
22. W. Miles, *Military Operations: France and Belgium, 1916. II. 2nd July 1916 to the End of the Battles of the Somme* (Macmillan, 1938)
23. P.A. Pedersen, 'The AIF on the Western Front' in *Australia in Two*

Centuries of War and Peace (AWM, 1988)

24. P.A. Pedersen, *Monash as Military Commander* (MUP, 1992)

25. E. Pentreath, *History of the 59th Battalion AIF* (59 Bn Assoc, 1968)

26. F. Loraine Petre, *The Royal Berkshire Regiment. II. 1914-18* (Published by the Regiment, 1925)

27. J.J. Shannessy, *History of the 2/6th Royal Warwicks 1914-19* (Cornish Bros, 1929)

28. H. Sloan, *The Purple and Gold. A History of the 30th Battalion* (Sydney, 1938)

29. T. Travers, *The Killing Ground* (Allen & Unwin)

30. J. Willcocks, *With the Indians in France* (Leo Constable, 1920)

31. H. R. Williams, *The Gallant Company* (Angus & Robertson, 1933)

32. J.F. Williams, 'Words on a Lively Skirmish' in *Journal of the Australian War Memorial*, No.23, October, 1998

33. C. Wray, *Sir James Whiteside McCay* (Oxford, 2002)

INDEX

(Ranks are those held in July 1916)